Anonymous

Southwest Pacific Railroad Company

Anonymous

Southwest Pacific Railroad Company

ISBN/EAN: 9783744727198

Printed in Europe, USA, Canada, Australia, Japan

Cover: Foto ©Andreas Hilbeck / pixelio.de

More available books at **www.hansebooks.com**

RAILROAD COMPANY.

ATLANTIC & PACIFIC

RAILROAD COMPANY.

Statutes, Conveyances and Documents.

New-York :
STOCKHOLDER JOB PRINTING OFFICE,
72 William Street.
1867.

THWEST PACIFIC

ILROAD COMPANY.

NTIC & PACIF

AILROAD COMPANY.

Conveyances and Docume

New-York:

STOCKHOLDER JOB PRINTING OFFICE,

72 William Street.

1867.

CONTENTS.

ORGANIZATION

OF THE

SOUTHWEST PACIFIC RAILROAD COMPANY,

Under Act of General Assembly of Missouri, approved
March 20th, 1866.

CAPITAL STOCK,

80,000 Shares, $100 each, . . $8,000,000

Mortgage Bonds. . . . $7,250,000

IN SUMS OF $1,000 EACH.

Issued at the rate of $25,000 per mile upon Completed Road.
Guaranteed by the "Atlantic and Pacific Railroad Company."

LENGTH OF ROAD.

Completed, ...	90 Miles
In progress, ...	200 "
	290 Miles

Number of Acres embraced in Land-Grant.

(One million two hundred and fifty thousand),	1,250,000
Of which there has been sold . .	200,000
BALANCE UNSOLD, . : ;	1,050,000 Acres

Embracing Agricultural and Mineral lands.

JANUARY, 1867.

OFFICERS

OF THE

SOUTHWEST PACIFIC RAILROAD COMPANY,

1866–'67.

BOARD OF DIRECTORS.

Gen'l JOHN C. FREMONT,	FREDERICK BILLINGS,
CHARLES H. WARD,	LEVI PARSONS,
E. F. BEALE,	J. P. ROBINSON,
JOSIAH CALDWELL,	JAMES TAUSSIG,
CHAS. ZAGONYI,	A. JACOBS,
J. J. GRAVELY,	S. H. BOYD,
GEORGE T. M. DAVIS.	

PRESIDENT:
Gen'l JOHN C. FREMONT,

VICE-PRESIDENT:
Hon. LEVI PARSONS,

TREASURER:
WILLIAM A. STEPHENS.

SECRETARY:
C. F. MANSON.

CHIEF ENGINEER:
J. P. ROBINSON,

SUPERINTENDENT:
WILLIAM A. PILE.

AGENT OF LAND DEPARTMENT:
A. ALBERT.

Office, 54 William Street, New-York.

ORGANIZATION

OF THE

ATLANTIC AND PACIFIC RAILROAD COMPANY,

Under Act of Congress approved July 27th, 1866.

CAPITAL STOCK,
$100,000,000,

One Million Shares, of 100 Dollars each.

Mortgage per mile to be regulated by Act of Congress.

LENGTH OF ROAD,   2,000 MILES.

Number of Acres embraced in Land-Grant.

(*Fifty-five millions*),   *55,000,000.*

JANUARY, 1867,

OFFICERS

OF THE

ATLANTIC AND PACIFIC RAILROAD COMPANY.

Gen'l JOHN C. FREMONT, New-York.
Hon. LEVI PARSONS,   "
PAUL S. FORBES,   "
HENRY H. WARD,   "
ROBERT L. CUTTING,   "
LEONARD W. JEROME,   "
CHARLES H. WARD,   "
J. P. ROBINSON,   "
CHARLES GOULD,   "
DANIEL R. GARRISON, St. Louis, Mo.
E. W. FOX.   "
FREDERICK BILLINGS, California.
L. L. ROBINSON,   "

PRESIDENT:
Gen'l JOHN C. FREMONT, New-York.

ASSISTANT PRESIDENT:
HON. LEVI PARSONS, New-York.

FIRST VICE-PRESIDENT:
DANIEL R. GARRISON, Missouri.

SECOND VICE-PRESIDENT:
L. L. ROBINSON, California.

SECRETARY:
CHARLES H. HOWLAND, Missouri.

TREASURER:
WM. A. STEPHENS, New-York.

Office, 54 William Street, New-York.

HISTORICAL MEMOIR

OF THE

SOUTHWEST PACIFIC RAILROAD.

PREVIOUS to 1850, little or no attention had been given to the subject of internal improvements in the State of Missouri. A Board of Improvement had been created in 1840, but nothing further was done than to make a survey for a railroad from St. Louis to the Iron Mountain, by the way of Big river, and some surveys of the Osage river, with a view of improving its navigation.

The subject of a railroad across the continent having been discussed in various quarters, for several years, Col. Benton, then United States Senator for Missouri, on the 7th of February, 1849, introduced a bill into the United States Senate to provide for the location and construction of a central national road from the Pacific ocean to the Mississippi river—to be an iron railway where practicable, and a wagon road where a railway was not practicable—and proposed to set apart seventy-five per cent. of the proceeds of the sales of the public lands in Oregon and California, and fifty per cent. of the proceeds of all other sales of the public lands, to defray the cost of its location and construction.

On the 20th February, a spirited public meeting was held at the court-house in St. Louis, and a series of resolutions, introduced by Thomas Allen, was adopted, requesting the Legislature, then in session, to grant a charter and right of way, &c.,

for a railway across the state, from St. Louis to the western boundary.

On the 12th of March, 1849, a charter was granted, providing for a capital of $10,000,000, and with "power to survey, mark, locate and construct a railroad from the city of St. Louis to the city of Jefferson; and thence to some point on the western line of Van Buren county, in this state, with a view that the same may be hereafter continued westwardly to the Pacific ocean." The corporators named in the charter were John O'Fallon, Louis V. Bogy, James H. Lucas, Edward Walsh, George Collier, Thomas B. Hudson, Daniel D. Page, Henry M. Shreve, James E. Yeatman, John B. Sarpy, Wayman Crow, Joshua B. Brant, Thomas Allen, Robert Campbell, Pierre Chouteau, Jr., Henry Shaw, Bernard Pratte, Ernst Angelrodt, Adolphus Meier, Louis A. Benoist and Adam L. Mills.

At this time not a single railroad touched St. Louis on either side of the Mississippi river, nor was any built in the vicinity. The Erie Railroad was not completed, and only 7,000 miles of railroad had been constructed in the United States. At that time there were large bodies of public land in the state open to private entry, 29,216,000 acres as was stated in the memorial to Congress, remaining unsold.

The following gentlemen were elected directors for the first year: Thomas Allen, James H. Lucas, D. D. Page, Edward Walsh, George Collier, James E. Yeatman, L. M. Kennett, Louis A. Labeaume and James Harrison. The preliminary surveys were commenced on the 24th May, and were closed on the 29th November, 1850.

Five different lines were surveyed, embracing in the whole over 800 miles of survey. Taking into consideration as well the estimated cost of construction of the different lines, as the probable need of a branch to the Iron Mountain, and to the southwest part of the state, the location, by Mill creek valley, valley of the River Des Peres, and by the valley of the Meramec, was adopted on the 18th of June, 1851.

The first division of the road (33 miles) having been put under contract, the first spadeful of earth was removed, in the absence of the governor, by the then mayor of the city, Mr. Kennett, on the 4th of July, in the presence of a large and enthusiastic audience, who were first addressed by the president and Hon. Edward Bates. This memorable event took place at a point on the south bank of Chouteau Pond, on Mr. Minckes' ground, west of Fifteenth street.

In the winter of 1850-'51, a plan for a complete system of railroads for the state was laid before the Legislature by Thomas Allen, president of the road, who had been elected to the state senate, and including a form of state aid by a loan of the public credit. This plan, which was soon adopted with some variation of starting points, contemplated the issue of state bonds to the railroad company to an amount equal to the amount first to be advanced by the stockholders, the company agreeing to pay the interest and principal of the bonds, and the state reserving a first lien on the road as security. The first act was approved February 22d, 1851, and provided for the issue to the extent of two millions of state bonds to the Pacific Railroad Company, in sums of $50,000, upon satisfactory evidence being furnished to the governor, at each application, that a like sum of $50,000 had been expended by the company, derived from sources other than state bonds; *and provided*, that the bonds should not be sold below par. These bonds having twenty years to run, and bearing six per cent. interest, were sold for a premium for more than a year and a half, and some were sold as high as 110. Some important amendments to the charter were granted at the same session, by an act approved March 1, 1851.

Congress, on the 10th June, 1852, passed an act granting to the state of Missouri the alternate sections of land in a strip six sections in width on each side of the line, for the construction of a railroad from St. Louis to the western boundary of the state. So largely, however, had individuals entered the public lands the previous year or two, in consequence of the railroad surveys, that it was found that the grant would be of little value for constructing a railroad in a direct line westward from St. Louis to the western boundary. Therefore, in view of the immense district of country lying at the south-west, known to be desirable in soil, climate and minerals, yet theretofore inaccessible, and also in view of the probability that a good route for the NATIONAL ROAD *to California* might be found along the 35th parallel, it was deemed advisable to make a fork in the line of road, and run one branch nearly west in the direction of Kansas, via the state capital, and the other fork in the southwestern direction. To the road from St. Louis to the point of divergence from the main line, and thence to the southwest boundary of the state, the state granted the lands by the act of December 20th, 1852, without bonus, and with an exemption from taxation until the road could pay a dividend; and with also a further loan of $1,000,000 to the Kansas branch, and $1,000,000 to the Southwest Road. The right of pre-emption to actual settlers already on the lands, at $2.50 per acre, was, however, reserved.

Mr. Allen, president of the company, was appointed the agent of the state to select the lands, and for that purpose he went to Washington City. The lands selected, and the schedule of which, as furnished by the General Land Office, has the force of a patent, amounted to about 1,200,000 acres.

About this time provision was made by law providing for a geological survey of the state, and $10,000 a year for two years was appropriated for that object. One of the consequences which has flowed from that law is, the accompanying interesting report of the state geologist, upon the geology of the country, rich in minerals, through which the Southwest Pacific Railroad is located.

It was on the 31st March, 1853, that Congress provided for such explorations and surveys as the War Department might deem advisable, in order to ascertain the most practicable and economical route for a railroad from the Mississippi river to the Pacific Ocean. Very soon after, Mr. Allen, being then in Washington, and believing a route in that direction practicable, proposed to the Secretary of War to make a survey, without expense to the government, for a railroad through southwestern Missouri, and thence by the way of the Canadian river and Albuquerque, &c., to California, which route has been since travelled in part for some years by the overland mail.

In 1852, Thomas S. O'Sullivan, Esq., having been elected chief engineer, on the resignation of Mr. Kirkwood, the Southwest Branch was surveyed and located, under the immediate charge of his assistant, James K. Ford, Esq.

In July, 1853, the first division was opened from St. Louis to Franklin, thirty-eight miles. In the spring of that year, the president being then in New York, a contract was made with Diven, Stancliff & Co., for the construction of the whole Southwestern Road. A meeting of stockholders was held at Mercantile Library Hall, and it was proposed that the county of St. Louis make an additional subscription of $1,200,000 to the capital stock of the company, to be paid by taxation within four years, and that the stockholders claim no exemption from the tax, as the law allowed, in consequence of their being already subscribers. At the election which took place, on the question of making the subscription and levying the heavy tax proposed on the part of the county of St. Louis, it was decided affirmatively by a vote of 3420 yeas to 1133 nays. Thus the people of St. Louis made themselves the first example in the state under the law authorizing the imposition of taxes for railroad purposes.

On the resignation of Mr. Allen, HUDSON E. BRIDGE, Esq., was elected president April 25, 1854. The work was pushed forward on all the contracts to Jefferson City in 1855; and in September, the work under the contract for Southwestern Road was also commenced.

A law was passed on the 7th of December, 1855, to secure the prompt payment of the interest on the state bonds, by requiring the setting apart out of the state treasury, on the 1st July, 1856, the sum of $200,000 as a basis of a state interest fund, and the further sum of $100,000 annually for thirteen years. The treasurer and auditor of the state were made commissioners of this fund; and in case any railroad company failed to deposit with the treasury of the state a sufficient sum to meet the interest upon any state bonds loaned to them thirty days before the interest becomes due, the auditor is required to pay out of the fund to the treasurer a sum sufficient to pay the interest as it falls due, such sum to be refunded by the delinquent railroad company, under penalty of receiving no more bonds and forfeiting their road to the state.

The security of the state, being the first lien, was based not only upon the roads themselves and their appurtenances, but also upon large grants of land, amounting to over two millions of acres, of which the fee simple title has absolutely passed by act of Congress and the decision of the general land office. For a breach of the conditions of the acts under which state aid was granted to the several roads, the sale of several, among them the Southwest Branch, now known as the Southwest Pacific Railroad, was decreed by statutes of the state, the text of which is hereto subjoined. The various documents connected with the sale of the road and its transfer to the present Southwest Pacific Railroad Company are also herewith printed.

Inasmuch as this road is to become and to be known as the Missouri Division of the Atlantic and Pacific Railroad, chartered by act of Congress approved July 27th, 1866, the guaranty of the latter company has been affixed to the bonds of the South-west Pacific Railroad. The broader land grant of the Atlantic and Pacific Company, ten alternate sections on either side of the road within the limits of Missouri and twenty sections from the western boundary of the state to the Pacific ocean, covers a portion of the route of the Southwest Pacific in Missouri. In view of which the names of the officers and board of directors of the former company are published herewith, the organization having been fully completed in accordance with the act of Congress and certificate thereof filed in the Department of the Interior, according to the requirements of the statute. The preliminary steps for a merger of the two companies have already been taken. The land grant in aid of the construction of the Atlantic and Pacific Company embraces about 55,000,000 acres in Missouri, the Indian Territory, New Mexico, Arizona and California. The route enters and passes along the zone of fertile land which, as the thirty-fourth parallel of latitude is approached, extends some 350 miles farther west than such land is found to the northward of that vicinity, even to the forty-ninth parallel of latitude, where the ninety-seventh meridian is the general western limit of the arable belt. The Missouri Division of this great line between the Missouri river at St. Louis and the Pacific, as well from its local as from its contemplated through traffic, must be deemed one of the most valuable sections of railway in the country. For the business of the region it serves it nowhere encounters competition from navigable waters; and having been a favored line in Missouri, the recipient of aid both in money and lands, it may be said, so far as parallel or rival projects are concerned, that very many years must elapse before even the boldest projectors will seek to confront the formidable expenditure already represented in the cash and land capital of the road.

CHAPTER XLV.

An Act granting the Right of Way to the State of Missouri, and a portion of the Public Lands, to aid in the construction of certain Railroads in said State.

Be it enacted by the Senate and House of Representatives of the United States of America, in Congress assembled:

That the right of way through the public lands be, and the same is hereby granted to the State of Missouri, for the construction of railroads from the town of Hannibal to the town of St. Joseph, in said state, and from the city of St. Louis to such point on the western boundary of said state, as may be designated by the authority of said state, with the right also to take necessary materials of earth, stone and timber for the construction thereof from the public lands of the United States adjacent to said railroads ; *provided*, that in locating the railroads aforesaid, and assigning the limits to the easement, no more land shall be taken from the United States than is necessary for a convenient construction and use of said roads as public ways for transportation, including stations, with the usual buildings of all kinds, turnouts and such other appurtenances as are usually enjoyed by railroad companies, and a copy of the location of said roads, made under the direction of the Legislature, shall be forwarded to the proper local land offices respectively, and to the general land office at Washington city, within ninety days after the completion of the same, to be recorded.

Sec. 2. *And be it further enacted,* That there be and is hereby granted to the State of Missouri, for the purpose of aiding in making the railroads aforesaid, every alternate section of land designated by even numbers, for six sections in width on each side of said road ; but in case it shall appear that the United States have, when the line or route of said roads, or either of them, shall be definitely fixed by the authority aforesaid, sold any section or any part thereof granted as aforesaid, or that the right of pre-emption has attached to the same, then it shall be lawful for any agent or agents to be appointed by the governor of said state, to select, subject to the approval of the Secretary of the Interior, from the lands of the United States most contiguous to the tier of sections above specified, so much land in alternate sections, or parts of sections, as shall be equal to such lands as the United States have sold, or to which the right of pre-emption has attached as aforesaid; which lands, thus selected in lieu of those sold, and to which pre-emption rights have attached as aforesaid, together with the sections and parts of sections designated by even numbers as aforesaid, and appropriated as aforesaid, shall be held by the State of Missouri for the use and purposes aforesaid; *provided* that the lands to be so located shall in no case be further than fifteen miles from the line of the road in each case; *provided further*, that the lands hereby granted shall be exclusively applied in the construction of that road for which it was granted and selected, and shall be disposed of only as the work progresses, and the same shall be applied to no other purpose whatsoever; *and provided further*, that any and all lands heretofore reserved to the United States by any act of Congress, or in any other manner by competent authority, for the purpose of aiding in any object of internal improvement, or for any other purpose whatsoever, be and the same are hereby reserved to the United States from the operation of this act, except so far as it may be found necessary to locate the route of the said railroads through such reserved lands, in which case the right of way only shall be granted.

Sec. 3. *And be it further enacted,* That the sections and parts of sections of land which, by such grant, shall remain to the United States, within six miles on each side of said roads, shall not be sold for less than double the minimum price of the public lands when sold; which lands shall from time to time be offered at public sale to the highest bidder, under the direction of the Secretary of the Interior, and shall not be subject to entry until they shall have been so offered at public sale.

Sec. 4. *And be it further enacted,* That the said lands hereby granted to the said state shall be subject to the disposal of the Legislature thereof for the purposes aforesaid, and no other; and the said railroads shall be and remain public highways for the use of the government of the United States, free from toll or other charge upon the transportation of any property or troops of the United States.

SEC. 5. *And be it further enacted,* That the lands hereby granted to said state shall be disposed of by said state only in manner following, that is to say: that a quantity of land not exceeding one hundred and twenty sections on each road, and included within a continuous length of twenty miles of said road, may be sold; and when the governor of said state shall certify to the Secretary of the Interior that said twenty miles of said road is completed, then another like quantity of land hereby granted may be sold; and so from time to time, until said road is completed; and if said road be not completed within ten years, no further sales shall be made, and the land unsold shall revert to the United States.

SEC. 6. *And be it further enacted,* That the United States mail shall at all times be transported on said railroads under the direction of the Post Office Department, at such price as Congress may by law direct.

Approved June 10th, 1852.

CHAPTER XCVII.

An Act supplemental to "An Act granting the Right of Way to the State of Missouri, and a portion of the Public Lands to aid in the construction of certain Railroads in said State," approved June tenth, eighteen hundred and fifty-two.

Be it enacted by the Senate and House of Representatives of the United States of America in Congress assembled, That the time required by the act to which this is supplemental, for the completion of the road therein described, "from the city of St. Louis to such point on the western boundary of said state as may be designated by the authority of said state," as well as the time of reversion to the United States of the lands thereby granted to the state of Missouri for the use of said road, is hereby extended for ten years, from the tenth day of June, eighteen hundred and sixty-two: *provided,* that in case said company fail to complete said road within the time as thus extended, the said lands shall then revert to the United States.

Approved June 5th, 1862.

AN ACT

To accept a grant of land made to the State of Missouri by the Congress of the United States, to aid in the construction of certain Railroads in this State, and to apply a portion thereof to the Pacific Railroad.

Be it enacted by the General Assembly of the State of Missouri as follows :

SEC. 1. That all that portion of the lands granted to this state by the act of Congress, entitled, "An act granting the right of way to the state of Missouri, and a portion of the public lands to aid in the construction of certain railroads in said state," approved June 10th, 1852, so far as the same are applicable to the construction of a railroad from the city of St. Louis to such point on the western boundary of this state as may be designated by the Pacific Railroad (Company), and which may be selected or located in conformity with the provisions of said act, together with all the rights and privileges thereto belonging or in said act granted, shall vest in full and complete title in the Pacific Railroad (Company), for the uses and purposes, and subject to the conditions, reversion and provisions set forth and contained in said act of Congress and in this act.

SEC. 2. The Pacific Railroad (Company) may lay out, construct and maintain a line of railway, or branch railroad, with a single or double track, from any point on the main line of the Pacific Railroad east of the Osage River, to any point on the western boundary of this state, south of the Osage River, which the said corporation may select, and for that purpose shall have the same rights, powers and privileges, and be subject to the same provisions and conditions in respect to the right of way, depot grounds, water stations, engine houses, machine shops, stopping stages, and other buildings, and the use of materials, and the location, construction, maintaining and operation of the said branch railroad as are made applicable to the Pacific Railroad, by the act entitled "An act to incorporate the Pacific Railroad," approved March 12th, 1849, and the act amendatory thereof, approved March 1st, 1851.

Sec. 3. As soon as practicable after the passage of this act, the Pacific Railroad (Company) shall, at their own expense, proceed to locate said southwestern line or branch railroad, and to locate and select the lands granted by the said act of Congress, by any agent or agents they may designate, under the appointment of the governor, subject to the approval in said act specified, along the main line of said Pacific Railroad, from its commencement in the city of St. Louis to the point on said main line where the said Southwestern Branch shall diverge, and thence along said southwestern line or branch railroad to the western boundary, south of the Osage River. And a copy of the location of the aforesaid part of the main line and of the whole of said Southwestern Branch of the Pacific Railroad shall be made and certified by the president and chief engineer of said railroad, and under the corporate seal of said company, and forwarded to the local land offices, and to the general land office, as in said act of Congress specified.

Sec. 4. And the said Pacific Railroad shall apply the lands granted as aforesaid, or the proceeds thereof, to the construction of the said main line, from its commencement in the city of St. Louis to the point of divergence therefrom of the said Southwestern Branch, and to the said Southwestern Branch, so that said lands shall be applied to the construction of a railroad from St. Louis to the western boundary of the state, south of the Osage River, in conformity with said act of Congress.

Sec. 5. For the purpose of raising funds from time to time, for the construction and completion of the said branch railroad, the said company may sell the said lands in the manner provided for by the said act of Congress, and may issue their bonds in such sums as they may deem proper, at rates of interest not exceeding seven per cent. per annum, payable semi-annually, and the principal of said bonds payable at such time and place as they may designate; and may secure the payment of said bonds by mortgage of said lands, or any part thereof, to be executed by said company, and may make the said bonds convertible into land or stock of the company within such periods as they may prescribe; *provided*, that the faith of the state is in no manner pledged for the redemption of said bonds or any part thereof; *and provided further,* that nothing in this act contained shall be construed to authorize said company to sell, dispose of, or apply the said lands, or the proceeds thereof, in any other manner or to any other purpose than as required and limited by the said act of Congress.

SEC. 6. The said company shall, within one year after the said Southwestern Branch Railroad shall have been located, cause to be made a map and profile thereof, and a map of the land located for the use of said branch road, embracing also the main line of the Pacific Railroad from its connection with said Southwestern Branch to the eastern terminus thereof, and file the same in the office of the secretary of state, and also maps of the parts thereof located in the different counties, and cause the same to be recorded in the office for recording deeds in the counties respectively in which said parts of said road may be located.

SEC. 7. Each and every person who, on the tenth day of June, one thousand eight hundred and fifty-two, was the owner of any improvement made previous to that date on any land embraced in the grant aforesaid, and who became such owner with a view to a residence on, or occupation of such land, for agricultural purposes, shall have the right to purchase at not exceeding two dollars and fifty cents per acre, subject to the reversion in said act provided for, a quantity of the land so occupied, to be bounded by the legal sub-divisions, not exceeding one quarter section, to consist of quarter quarter, half quarter or quarter section, which will include the improvement aforesaid; *provided*, that any person claiming the right to purchase under the provisions of this act, shall, within four months from the date of the location of the land, file in the clerk's office of the circuit court of the county in which the land claimed is situated, a notice to the said corporation of his, her or their claims, describing the land by its numbers, accompanied with an affidavit stating the date and object of the improvement, the time and manner when and how he, she or they became owner thereof, and also the affidavits of at least two residents of the county, proving the facts in relation to such claim; *and provided further*, that the right of way upon and across any lot of land sold under the provisions of this section, not exceeding two hundred feet in width, shall be reserved and retained for the passage of the road, as the same may be located and constructed; but no sale or conveyance of any lot of land under the provisions of this section shall affect the rights or equities of two or more parties claiming the same as between each other.

*　　*　　*　　*　　*　　*　　*　　*

Sec. 12. The said Pacific Railroad and the said Southwestern Branch Railroad shall be exempt from taxation respectively, until the same shall be completed, opened and in operation, and shall declare a dividend, when the road bed, buildings, machinery, engines, cars and other property of such completed road, at the actual cash value thereof, shall be subject to taxation at the rate assessed by the state on other real and personal property of like value.

* * * * * * * *

Sec. 13. It shall be lawful for any city, county or incorporated company to subscribe to the capital stock of the said Pacific Railroad, for the purpose of aiding the construction of said railroad, or either of its branches, and may issue the bonds of such city, county or company, to raise funds to pay the stock thus subscribed, and appoint an agent to represent its interest, give its vote, and receive its dividends, and may take proper steps to guard and protect the interest of such city, county or corporation in relation thereto.

This act shall take effect and be in force from and after its passage.

Approved December 25th, 1852.

AN ACT

To secure the completion of certain Railroads in this State (Missouri).

* * * * * * *

Sec. 28. In case the Pacific Railroad fails to complete the said first division of said Southwest Branch in three years from the passage of this act, or to pay the interest on said guaranteed bonds, or to hold the state harmless from said guarantee, then, and in that case, the said Southwest Branch Railroad, the lands appropriated to the construction thereof, belonging to the railroad company at the time of such default, and all appurtenances and franchises, shall at once, by operation of law, and without any process or proceeding, become the property of the state, subject only to the aforesaid mortgage. And the governor of this state, upon the failure of said company to perform all or either of the above conditions, may take possession thereof in behalf of the state, and manage and control the same until otherwise disposed of by act of the Legislature.

* * * * , * *

Passed December 10th, 1855.

STATE OF MISSOURI.

AN ACT

To provide for the Sale of certain Railroads and Property by the
Governor, to foreclose the State's lien thereon, and to secure
an early completion of the Southwest Branch Pacific, the
Platte Country, the St. Louis and Iron Mountain, and the
Cairo and Fulton Railroads, of Missouri.

[Approved February 19, 1866.]

*Be it enacted by the General Assembly of the State of Missouri,
as follows :—*

SECTION 1. The Governor is hereby directed and required to
take immediate possession of the Southwest Branch of the Pacific
Railroad, together with all the appurtenances, real estate, rolling
stock, cars, engines, depots and other property, real or personal,
and all rights and franchises thereunto attached or in anywise
belonging, as is provided by law, and the said railroad, together
with all the lands heretofore appropriated to the construction of
said railroad, and belonging to the Pacific Railroad Company
for the use and benefit of said Southwest Branch, at the time of
its default, as provided by the act entitled " An act to accept a
" grant of land made to the State of Missouri by the Congress of
"the United States, to aid in the construction of certain rail
" roads in this State, and to apply a portion thereof to the Pacific
" Railroad," approved December 25, 1852, and all other acts
relating to said Southwest Branch, and all the appurtenances
and franchises thereunto attached, having become the property
of this State by operation of law, it shall be the duty of the
governor to do all things necessary and proper by him to be
done to secure the same to this state free from all claims or
incumbrances of all other claimants whomsoever, and upon
obtaining such possession the governor shall turn said road and
the other property and assets aforesaid over to a board of com-

missioners hereinafter created, by them to be operated and sold in the interest of the state according to the terms and conditions of this act. It shall be the further duty of the governor to advertise the St. Louis and Iron Mountain Railroad, the Cairo and Fulton Railroad of Missouri, and the Weston and Atchison, Atchison and St. Joseph, and Platte Country Railroads, and every part and section of each of said roads, as far as the same are constructed or projected, together with their appurtenances, rolling stock, and property of every description, and all rights and franchises thereto belonging, for sale, and to sell the same at auction to the highest bidder, in pursuance of the provisions of the several acts creating a lien on said railroads, their appurtenances, rights and franchises in favor of the state. The said Weston and Atchison, Atchison and St. Joseph, and the Platte Country Railroads shall be known and designated hereinafter, and after the passage of this act, as the Platte Country Railroad. The said Southwest Branch of the Pacific Railroad shall be known and designated hereafter as the Southwest Pacific Railroad.

Sec. 2. A Board of Commissioners composed of three members, who shall be nominated by the governor and confirmed by the senate, is hereby established for each of said railroads, viz: The Southwest Branch of the Pacific Railroad, the St. Louis and Iron Mountain Railroad, the Cairo and Fulton Railroad of Missouri, and the Platte Country Railroad. A majority of the members of each board shall at all times constitute a quorum for the transaction of business; and in case of a vacancy occurring in said boards, such vacancy shall be filled by appointment by the governor, subject to the confirmation of the senate at its next session thereafter. Said commissioners shall, before entering on the discharge of their duties, take and subscribe the same oath prescribed for other state officers. They shall each enter into bond, with such security and such amount as the governor shall from time to time order and approve, conditioned for the faithful performance of their duties under the law. They may employ counsel and such agents and assistants as they may require in the performance of their duties. They shall account for and pay over to the state treasurer all moneys that may come into their hands belonging to the state, whether derived from the sale or the net earnings of the respective roads, taking duplicate receipts therefor, one of which shall be deposited with the state auditor. They shall make quarterly reports to the governor of their proceedings, and a final report of all matters relating to the interests and trusts confided to them, immediately after the sale of their respective roads. And all letters, bids, proposals, oaths, bonds, books, papers and other documents that come into their hands, or into the hands of the governor, or which they have executed to the state, shall be deposited with the secretary of state. And they and their employees shall receive such compensation, besides necessary expenses, for their services as the governor from time to time may allow and certify to the auditor, who shall audit such allowance and draw his warrant for the same, to be paid out of any funds in the treasury not otherwise appropriated; *provided*, that the amount allowed for services shall not exceed in the aggregate one thousand dollars to each commissioner. All vacancies in any board of commissioners shall be certified to the governor by the remaining commissioner or commissioners within twenty days after such vacancy occurs.

Sec. 3. It shall be the duty of the boards of commissioners appointed for the Southwest Branch of the Pacific Railroad, and the Platte Country Railroad, to receive possession of said roads, appurtenances, lands, choses in action and other property belonging thereto, from the hands of the governor, and to manage, operate, and dispose of the same in the manner and for the purpose provided in this act. It shall also be the duty of the commissioners respectively appointed for the St. Louis and Iron Mountain Railroad, the Cairo and Fulton Railroad of Missouri, and the Platte Country Railroad, to attend the sale of their respective roads as advertised by the governor, and to bid in the same for the use and benefit of the state, for an amount not exceeding the respective liens on said roads in favor of the state. And if said roads, or either of them, are struck off and sold to said commissioners, they shall take possession and hold the same, with their appurtenances and property; manage, operate and dispose of the same in the manner provided for in this act.

Sec. 4. Within thirty days after they shall have been appointed and qualified, the respective boards of commissioners aforesaid shall publish a notice of their appointment as such; of their authority to take possession of or to buy in said roads, together with the lands belonging to their respective roads, and again to sell the same; and they shall invite proposals for the purchase of their respective roads, lands and appurtenances and franchises from said commissioners. The notice in relation to the Southwest Branch Railroad shall be published for at least sixty days. The notices in relation to the St. Louis and Iron Mountain Railroad, the Cairo and Fulton Railroad, and the Platte Country Railroad, shall each be published in conjunction with the respective notices of sale of said roads required by the first section of this act to be published by the governor. They shall be published in the same manner, in the same newspapers, for the same time, and for sixty days thereafter. All such notices shall be published in at least two newspapers in the cities of St. Louis, New York, Philadelphia, and Boston.

Sec. 5. The proposals of bidders, under the provisions of the foregoing section, shall each state the price bid for the respective roads, and shall state that they are based on the following terms and conditions, which are hereby established to govern the sale of said roads by said boards of commissioners:—*First*. The price or consideration bid shall be payable as follows: One-fourth on closing the contract, and the balance in five equal annual installments; the first installment payable in one year, the second in two, the third in three, the fourth in four, and the fifth in five years thereafter, with six per cent. interest on deferred payments, payable annually; *provided*, that all sums bid may be paid at any time, in either cash or the bonds or other liabilities of the state, or bonds guaranteed by the state. *Second*. The roads and all rolling stock belonging thereto shall be kept in good serviceable condition during the progress of the work to completion of said roads. *Third*. The Southwest Branch of the Pacific Railroad shall be finished to a point opposite the town of Lebanon, in Laclede county, within three years; to the town of Springfield, in Greene county, within four years; and to the western line of the state in five years after the date of sale; and the purchaser shall expend at least five hundred thousand dollars in each and every year between the date of sale and date fixed for the completion aforesaid in the work upon the graduation, masonry or superstructure of said extension. The St. Louis and Iron Mountain Railroad shall be finished to a point south of Pilot Knob, to connect with the Cairo and Fulton Railroad line, in three years, and finished to the Mississippi river, opposite to or below Columbus, Kentucky, in five years after the date of sale of said road ; and the purchasers of said road shall expend in each and every year between the date of sale and the completion of the road, at least the sum of five hundred thousand dollars in the work of graduation, masonry or superstructure on said extension. And the Cairo and Fulton Railroad of Missouri shall be completed from the Mississippi river, opposite the town of Cairo, Illinois, or Columbus, Kentucky, to the intersection of the St. Louis and Iron Mountain Railroad line, within three years after the date of sale thereof. The Platte Country Railroad aforesaid shall be finished from a point on the Missouri river, opposite the city of Kansas, to the city of Weston, and from Savannah to Forest City, in two years from the date of sale, and shall be completed to the Iowa state line in three years thereafter ; and the purchaser of said road shall expend, in each and every year between the date of sale and the time fixed for the completion aforesaid, in graduation, masonry and superstructure of said road, the sum of at least two hundred and fifty thousand dollars ; *provided*, that the faithful annual expenditures required in this section shall entitle the respective companies to an extension of time of payment of principal of purchase money due that year until two years after maturity of last installment ; *and provided*, that an annual statement of expenditures on each road shall be made, under oath, by the treasurer and two directors thereof, and filed with the secretary of state.

SEC. 6. On the day named in the respective notices of sale of said roads, by said commissioners, the respective boards shall proceed to compare the several bids and proposals by them received, and shall, as soon thereafter as is practicable, award the roads and every part and section thereof, their franchises and appurtenances, and all lands and other property, real and personal, to the highest and best bidders, whose bids are made in compliance with the terms and conditions of the foregoing sections of this act; *provided*, that the governor shall approve said awards ; *and provided further*, that all proposals may be rejected if the commissioners deem them unsatisfactory.

SEC. 7. In case all the bids for any road are declared unsatisfactory, as provided in the preceding section, notices of sale shall be renewed from time to time, and shall be published, in conformity with the requirements heretofore provided for, for three

months, and the same proceedings shall be had in relation to proposals, comparison of bids and awards, and all other matters
relating thereto, as is hereinbefore provided for, until a sale of all
said roads is effected; *provided*, that if, in the opinion of the
governor, the interest of the state will be promoted, and a more
expeditious and advantageous sale secured thereby, and work on
said Southwest Branch Railroad be more speedily commenced,
he shall direct, in writing, the commissioners for said road to sell
said road and all its lands, property, franchises and appurtenances,
at private sale, without notice of sale as herein required, on such
conditions as to the payment of the purchase money, the mode
of completion, and the rights of the purchaser to borrow money
for the completion of said road, as the parties contracting may
agree upon; *provided, however*, that no sale, under the provisions of this section, shall be made which shall not preserve to
the state a lien for the amount of purchase money remaining unpaid, or which shall not secure the completion of the Southwest
Pacific Railroad to a point opposite the town of Lebanon, in
Laclede county, within three years; to the town of Springfield,
in Greene county, within four years; and to the western line of
the state within five years after the date of sale; or which shall
not secure the expenditure of at least five hundred thousand
dollars each year in the construction and equipment of said road
until the same is completed; *and provided, however*, no sale
made shall be completed until first approved by the governor.

Section 8. Whenever and as soon as an award is made and
approved under either of the foregoing sections, the commissioners and the purchasers shall execute in duplicate a contract
embracing all the terms, stipulations and conditions to be performed by either party, and on which such sales and purchases
are made; which duplicate agreements shall be approved by the
governor, and one copy filed with the secretary of state; and
thereupon the Governor shall, in the name and on behalf of the
state, execute and deliver to such purchasers a formal deed of
conveyance, under the great seal of the state, which shall be construed as other deeds conveying real estate, and shall have the
effect to convey, transfer and make over to the purchasers said
road and all of the franchises, privileges, rights, title and interests appertaining to the road so sold, all roads, road beds, rolling
stock, machine shops and all other property, both real and per-

sonal, of every description, belonging or in any wise appertaining thereto; and in the case of the Southwest Branch of the Pacific Railroad, all the lands granted by the United States to the State of Missouri by act of Congress approved June 10, 1852, and by the State of Missouri granted to the said Pacific Railroad for the construction of the said Southwest Branch, by an act approved Dec. 25, 1852, which have been forfeited to the state; and the purchasers shall execute and deliver to the State of Missouri mortgages on said roads, franchises, lands and property aforesaid, as is required by this act to secure the payment of the purchase money; *provided*, that nothing in this act shall be so construed as to convey or to authorize the commissioners to convey to the purchasers of the Cairo and Fulton Railroad any of the lands subscribed by counties to the stock of said road.

SECTION 9. The companies or persons purchasing any of the above named roads, or either of them, shall have all the rights, franchises, privileges and immunities which were had and enjoyed by the companies for whose default said roads were sold, under the charter and the laws amendatory thereof; subject, however, to the conditions and limitations therein contained, and not inconsistent with the provisions of this act.

SECTION 10. The companies or persons purchasing the above named railroads, or either of them, under the provision of the 6th section of this act and the first part of the 7th section, which provides for a sale to the highest bidders, may have the privilege, and they are hereby authorized to borrow such sums of money for the completion of their respective roads, as contemplated by this act, or for the payment of the balance due the state or any part thereof, on such terms and at such rate of interest as they may deem expedient, and for that purpose they may issue construction bonds in denomination of five hundred or one thousand dollars, as they think proper, and to secure the payment of which they may execute in due form their respective mortgages on said roads, appurtenances and rolling stock, subject only, however, to the state's lien for the amount of the purchase money remaining unpaid. Said bonds shall be prepared by said companies, and on the back of each bond shall be printed this law, and in connection therewith shall be indorsed or printed a certificate, which shall be signed by the governor and countersigned by the secretary of state, under the seal of the state, to the effect that such bond is issued by authority of this act, and secured by a mortgage on the road and appurtenances and lands as aforesaid; the number of miles finished, the amount of the state's lien, and the amount expended by said company in the extension shall also be embraced in said certificate; but such indorsement shall in no wise be construed into any liability on the part of the state for the payment of said bonds or any part thereof. Said bonds shall be numbered and registered in the office of the secretary of state and delivered to said companies as follows: Whenever the sum of one hundred thousand dollars has been in good faith expended and paid out in cash on the work of extending either of said roads, as herein provided, since the purchase thereof, or since the last application for bonds, and the acting president, treasurer and chief engineer of said road shall file in the office of the secretary of state their certificate to that effect, verified to the satisfaction of the governor, by their affidavit, then the governor shall cause one hundred and twenty-five thousand dollars of said bonds to be endorsed and delivered to said company, who shall receipt to the secretary of state therefor. Said bonds may be delivered in larger amounts at any single application, *provided* the expenditures in cash on which such application is based bear the same ratio to the bonds issued as is established above; *provided further*, that expenditures in cash on account of the Cairo and Fulton Railroad, and the Platte Country Railroad extension to the amount of fifty thousand dollars or over, shall entitle them to bonds in the same ratio of amount: *provided further*, that the books, papers and vouchers of said companies shall always be subject to the inspection of the governor or his agent appointed therefor, and any evidence of bad faith in the application for bonds or in the representation of amounts of expenditures, until-removed or obviated to the satisfaction of the governor, shall be sufficient cause for the suspension of further delivery of bonds; *and provided*, that no lien shall be created on said road or appurtenances and rolling stock in any other manner than as allowed in this act, prior to the completion of said roads, respectively; but all such prohibited liens shall be null and void.

SECTION 11. The act approved March 2d, 1861, entitled "an act concerning the bonds of the Pacific Railroad guaranteed by the state," shall remain in force, and the state hereby assumes the full payment of such guaranteed bonds not exchanged, as provided for in said act, and will hold said company purchasing the Southwest Branch Railroad and the Pacific Railroad Company's main line harmless on account of said outstanding bonds, and the governor shall take all steps necessary and advisable to carry into effect the foregoing terms. When the company purchasing the said road shall have constructed, and in running order, twenty miles of said road extending on their line west of Rolla, and shall exhibit satisfactory proof thereof to the governor of the state, in order that said company may be enabled to make title to such lands as they are authorized to sell, it is hereby made the duty of the governor to issue the necessary certificate to the Secretary of the Interior, as provided for in section five of the act of Congress entitled " an act granting the right of way to the State of Missouri, and a portion of the public lands to aid in the construction of certain railroads in said state," approved June 10, 1852 ; *provided*, that nothing in this act shall be construed so as to impair in any manner the rights of any person to a pre-emption on any of the lands of the said Southwest Branch Railroad acquired under former or existing laws, and any action or proceedings in law, which may be commenced by said commissioners before a sale, shall be continued after a sale in their names for the benefit of the purchaser.

SEC. 12. It shall be the duty of the commissioners for the Southwest Branch Road to ascertain the quantity of land sold by said Pacific Railroad Company prior to March 3d, 1861, which had been granted to said company to aid in construction of said Southwest Branch, the price for which the same was sold, the names of the purchasers, and the quantity and description of the land purchased by each, and the amount of money received by said company on account of such sales ; and it shall be the duty of said commissioners to require all money so received by said company, and not heretofore paid to the treasurer of the state, as required by law, to be at once paid into the treasury of the state ; and in all cases where the said company have received the purchase money for any such lands, it is hereby made the duty of the treasurer of the state to execute to such purchaser a deed to said lands, signed by himself, and acknowledged before the secretary of state, who shall certify the same under the seal of his office.

Sec. 13. In the case of the Southwest Pacific Railroad, said commissioners shall have the power, and it is made their duty, to investigate and arrange all matters of account between the said Branch Railroad and the other Pacific Railroad line, and for this purpose they shall have access to the books and papers of the Pacific Railroad Company, and they shall have power to institute and prosecute all suits and other proceedings authorized by law to recover from said Pacific Railroad Company any balance which may be found due and owing from said Pacific Railroad Company to or on behalf of said Southwest Branch, or otherwise arrange the same as may be just and equitable; and said commissioners are hereby authorized, when put in possession of the said Southwest Branch, to negotiate, contract and adjust with the Pacific Railroad Company terms and conditions for business and running arrangements and connections, and do all things needed and proper to be done to continue to the owners of the said Southwest Branch the right of running their locomotives and cars from the town of Pacific, in Franklin county, to the city of St. Louis, for the transportation of freight and passengers in the interest and for the benefit of such owners of said Southwest Branch, to and from said points in the cars of the Southwest Pacific Railroad; and said commissioners are further empowered and directed to take all proper steps to adjust and determine the rights and relations existing between the Southwest Pacific Railroad and the residue of the railroad line of the Pacific Railroad Company and the rights and interests of the owners or managers of said railroad lines in the said railroad between the said town of Pacific and the city of St. Louis, and to do every thing which may be necessary to perpetuate to the said Southwest Branch a connection with the said city of St. Louis; and any contract, arrangement, or privilege which shall be negotiated or otherwise arranged by said commissioners for and on behalf of said Southwest Pacific Railroad, and the owners thereof, under and by virtue of the foregoing provisions, shall pass and inure to the purchaser or purchasers of said Southwest Branch.

Sec. 14. Any failure on behalf of said companies, or either of them, to pay the purchase money, or to expend the sums of money which by the terms of this act or by the terms of any contract herein called for are required to be annually expended in the work of extending and completing said roads respectively, shall work a forfeiture of said roads so in default, their franchises, rolling stock, appurtenances and other property, both real and personal, which belong to said companies respectively, to the State of Missouri; and in such case the governor shall proceed at once to take possession of the same, without the aid of any writ or process of law, if in his opinion it would be to the interest of the state; and shall hold and operate the same, through such agents as he may appoint therefor, until the General Assembly shall otherwise dispose of the same for the purpose of foreclosing the state's lien or mortgage.

SEC. 15. In the case of the sale of the St. Louis and Iron Mountain Railroad, it shall be made a condition of sale that the Legislature shall have, and reserves, the power from time to time to regulate the price of freight on iron ore and coal.

SEC. 16. All acts and parts of acts inconsistent with the provisions of this act are hereby repealed.

SEC. 17. This act shall take effect and be in force from and after its passage.

Approved, February 19, 1866.

STATE OF MISSOURI.

AN ACT

Supplementary to and explanatory of an Act entitled "An Act to provide for the sale of certain railroads and property by the Governor, to foreclose the State's lien thereon, and to secure an early completion of the Southwest Branch Pacific, the Platte Country, the St. Louis and Iron Mountain, and the Cairo and Fulton Railroads of Missouri."

[Approved March 19, 1866.]

Be it enacted by the General Assembly of the State of Missouri, as follows:

SECTION 1. Whenever in said acts the "Southwest Branch" or "Southwest Branch of the Pacific Railroad" are used, they shall be held to mean the same road designated in the first section of said act, as the Southwest Pacific Railroad.

SECTION 2. The fourth section of said act shall not be construed to require any new advertisement on the part of the governor, of any railroad he may have advertised under the law creating liens on railroads prior to the time of the appointment or organization of a board of commissioners for such road. But such sales, so advertised by the governor, shall proceed, without reference to the time of the insertion in the same papers of the notice by the commissioners.

SECTION 3. The tenth section of said act shall be so construed as to leave it optional with the purchaser or purchasers of any of said railroads issuing bonds under the provisions of said act, whether to print the said act and the certificate of the governor in full on the back of such bonds, or any part thereof, or to wholly omit the same, as such parties issuing such bonds may seem best; but said bonds shall be numbered and registered by the secretary of state, and his attestation thereof, under the seal of the state affixed thereto.

SECTION 4. Upon the production to the state treasurer of the certificate of the Pacific Railroad of the payment in full of the purchase money for any lands referred to in the twelfth section of said act, issued by said railroad prior to the date in said section mentioned, the state treasurer shall execute a deed as in said section required, and the register of lands shall preserve a record of such deeds. The said certificate of payment shall be filed and preserved by the state treasurer, and the commissioner for the Southwest Pacific Railroad may allow to the Pacific.Railroad such sum in their settlement with said railroad for expenditure in construction as they find has been faithfully expended out of the receipts from the sales of pre-empted lands ; *provided*, this act shall not be so construed as to grant deeds to any person who has not a clear right to such lands in accordance with the act of Congress, approved June 10th, 1852, which act prescribed the mode of disposing of said lands, and also in accordance with the provisions of the several acts of the Legislature of this state, having reference to the same.

SEC. 5. The fourth section of said act shall not be construed to require the commissioners to advertise notices of sale of said roads respectively in more than one newspaper in either city therein named ; nor to require them to commence the publication of such notices respectively, earlier than twenty days before the date fixed by the governor for the sale thereof to foreclose the state's lien; *provided*, that in all cases the notices shall be published at least sixty days.

SEC. 6. This act to take effect and be in force from and after its passage.

Approved March 19th, 1866.

STATE OF MISSOURI.

———————

AN ACT

Authorizing the Incorporation of the Purchaser or Purchasers of
any Railroad, or of any part, section or branch thereof, which
has heretofore, or may hereafter become forfeited to, and
sold by the State.

[Approved March 20, 1866.]

*Be it enacted by the General Assembly of the State of Missouri,
as follows:—*

SECTION 1. In case any railroad in this state has heretofore,
or may hereafter, become forfeited to the state, for any cause
now provided, or hereinafter to be provided, by law, or in case
any part, section or branch thereof, so forfeited, shall be sold by
the state or its agents, according to law; any individual or asso-
ciation of individuals who may become the purchaser or purchasers of said railroad, or of any part, section or branch thereof,
shall be authorized by this act to incorporate himself or themselves with a number of stockholders sufficient to make the
whole number of corporators at least thirteen, for the purpose
of taking possession of the property, real and personal, choses in
action, franchises, rights and privileges to him or them conveyed
or transferred by the state, in pursuance of such sale, and to
enable the said purchaser or purchasers and his or their associates to complete, furnish, equip, operate, manage and control
such road, or part, section or branch thereof, and the property,

franchises and appurtenances thereto belonging or in anywise appertaining.

SEC. 2. Said articles of incorporation shall state the name of the company, which name shall be that now fixed, or which may hereafter be fixed by law, as the name of such railroad, or part, section or branch thereof; and if no name be so affixed, then the name shall be designated by the corporators. Said articles shall also state the number of miles, if any, as near as may be, requisite to be built to complete such road, and the number of years the incorporation is to continue. They, said articles, shall also fix and determine the amount of the capital stock of said company, not exceeding ten millions of dollars, and the number of shares of which said capital stock shall consist; and they shall further state the name and places of residence of the directors of the company not less than five nor more than thirteen in number, who shall manage its affairs for the first year, and until others are chosen in their places. Each corporator named in said articles shall subscribe thereto his name, place of residence, and the number of shares of stock he agrees to take in said company.

SEC. 3. As soon as at least one thousand dollars of stock for every mile of railroad, necessary to be made to complete the road, shall have been subscribed, and five per cent. paid thereon in good faith and in cash to the directors named in said articles of incorporation, and as soon as these shall be indorsed thereon or annexed thereto, an affidavit, made by at least three of the directors named therein, that the amount of stock required by this section, has been in good faith subscribed, and five per cent. paid in cash thereon, as aforesaid, and that it is intended in good faith to complete or maintain and operate the road mentioned in said articles, then said articles of incorporation shall be filed in the office of the secretary of state, who shall endorse thereon the date of filing, and shall record the same in a book to be provided by him for that purpose, and from and after the day of the filing of said articles said company shall become and be a body corporate, empowered to act as such in all matters pertaining to the business thereof.

SEC. 4. Each corporation provided under this act shall have the same powers, franchises, rights and privileges, and be subject to the same liabilities and restrictions as the corporation to which it shall become the successor may have had and by its original charter and the amendments thereto, in, to and over the property and franchises, forfeited and sold as aforesaid, and the time and manner of electing directors of any corporation hereunder created or formed, the election or appointment of its officers, agents or servants, the enactment of by-laws, the transfer of stocks, the collection of unpaid balances of subscription to stock, and all other acts, which by such original charter and the amendments thereto have been or may hereafter be regulated shall be determined and regulated by and performed in accordance with said original charter and amendments thereto, except as herein otherwise provided.

SEC. 5. This act shall not be so construed as to deprive any purchaser or purchasers of the railroads, or parts, sections or branches thereof, mentioned and described in an act entitled "An Act to provide for the sale of certain railroads and property by the governor, to foreclose the state's lien thereon, to secure an early completion of the Southwest Branch Pacific, the Platte Country, the St. Louis and Iron Mountain, and the Cairo and Fulton Railroads, of Missouri," approved February 19, 1866, from any of the benefits, powers and privileges by said act conferred upon such purchaser or purchasers.

SEC. 6. Nothing in this act shall be so construed as to make it obligatory upon the purchaser or purchasers of any railroad, or part, section or branch thereof, which may be sold as aforesaid to incorporate under this or any other act of the Legislature, but such purchaser or purchasers may, if he or they see fit, proceed, without such incorporation, to take possession and control of, construct, manage and operate the same in accordance with the terms of this particular act, under which such railroad, or any part, section or branch thereof, may have been sold to him or them, and such purchaser or purchasers may avail himself or themselves of such corporate rights or franchises as he or they may have acquired by such purchase.

SEC. 7. Nothing in this act shall be so construed as to relieve the purchaser or purchasers of any of the railroads sold under the act in the preceding section mentioned, from the terms, conditions and limitations of such act.

SEC. 8. This act shall take effect and be in force from and after its passage.

Approved March 20, 1866.

NOTICE OF SALE

OF THE

SOUTHWEST PACIFIC RAILROAD.

(Heretofore called the Southwest Branch of the Pacific Railroad.)

OFFICE OF THE BOARD OF COMMISSIONERS FOR THE SOUTH-
WEST PACIFIC RAILROAD,
ST. LOUIS, MO., March 2, 1866.

The undersigned hereby give public notice that, in pursuance of an act of the General Assembly of the State of Missouri, entitled "An act to provide for the sale of certain railroads and property by the governor, to foreclose the state's lien thereon, and to secure an early completion of the Southwest Branch Pacific, the Platte Country, the St. Louis and Iron Mountain, and the Cairo and Fulton Railroads, of Missouri," approved February 19th, 1866, the undersigned have been duly appointed, confirmed, qualified and established a Board of Commissioners, under the terms and provisions of said act, with full authority to take possession of, manage and operate said Southwest Pacific Railroad, (heretofore called the Southwest Branch of the Pacific Railroad,) and to buy in and re-sell, or to sell and dispose of the same to others, with all and singular the lands heretofore appropriated to the construction of said railroad and belonging to the Pacific Railroad, for the use and benefit of said Southwest Branch, at the time of its default, as provided by the act of said General Assembly, entitled "An act to accept a grant of land made to the State of Missouri by the Congress of the United States, to aid in the construction of certain railroads in this state, and to apply a portion thereof to the Pacific Railroad," approved December 25th, 1852; also, with all and singular the rolling stock and other personal property, machine shops, depots, real estate, leasehold or other interest therein, and all the rights, privileges and franchises to said Southwest Pacific Railroad (heretofore known as said Southwest Branch of the Pacific Railroad) appertaining or in any wise belonging.

And the undersigned, commissioners as aforesaid, in further pursuance of the terms of said act, approved February 19th, 1866, do hereby invite written and sealed proposals for the purchase of said Southwest Pacific Railroad, (heretofore known as the Southwest Branch of the Pacific Railroad,) and all the other property, appurtenances, privileges and franchises aforesaid; in which proposals must be stated the price bid for the same, and that such proposal is based upon the following terms and conditions, viz:

First. The price or consideration bid, shall be payable as follows: One-fourth on closing the contract, and the balance in five equal annual installments; the first installment payable in one year, the second in two, the third in three, the fourth in four, and the fifth in five years thereafter, with six per cent. interest on deferred payments, payable annually; *provided* that all sums bid may be paid at any time in either cash or the bonds or other liabilities of the state, or bonds guaranteed by the state.

Second. The roads and all rolling stock belonging thereto, shall be kept in good serviceable condition during the progress of the work to completion of said roads.

Third. The said Southwest Pacific Railroad (formerly known as the Southwest Branch of the Pacific Railroad) shall be finished to a point opposite the town of Lebanon, in Laclede county, within three years; to the town of Springfield, in Greene county, within four years, and to the western line of the state in five years after the date of sale; and that if the bid be accepted, the bidder or bidders shall expend at least five hundred thousand dollars in each and every year between the date of sale and date fixed for the completion aforesaid, in the work upon the graduation, masonry or superstructure of said extension. *Provided,* that the faithful annual expenditures required as aforesaid, shall entitle the company to an extension of time of payment of principal of purchase money due, that year, until two years after maturity of last installment; and *provided,* that an annual statement of expenditures on the road shall be made under oath by the treasurer and two directors thereof, and filed with the secretary of state.

Proposals will be received until the 9th day of May, A. D. 1866.

They must be directed to P. Jos. Osterhaus, president of the board of commissioners of the Southwest Pacific Railroad, St. Louis, Mo., and indorsed "Proposals for purchase of Southwest Pacific Railroad."

Awards must be approved by the governor before they will be binding upon the state.

The undersigned commissioners, as aforesaid, reserve the right to reject any and all proposals not satisfactory.

Copies of the act, approved February 19th, 1866, under which this board is acting, can be obtained upon application to the commissioners.

As soon as practicable a catalogue of the rolling stock and personal property to be sold, will be issued, and can also be had upon application to the commissioners.

P. JOS. OSTERHAUS,
ROBT. J. McELHANEY,
A. W. MAUPIN.
Board of Commissioners.

St. Louis, March 2d, 1866.

PROPOSAL

OF

JOHN C. FREMONT.

𝕿𝕺 P. JOS. OSTERHAUS, ROBERT J. McELHANEY, and A. W. MAUPIN, Commissioners for the SOUTHWEST PACIFIC RAILROAD:

In pursuance of your notice, dated St. Louis, May 10th, 1866, inviting proposals to buy the Southwest Pacific Railroad and appurtenances at private sale, based upon the terms of the seventh section of the Act of the General Assembly of the State of Missouri, approved February 19th, 1866, I herewith make the following offer :—

1. I propose to buy under the provisions of said seventh section, for the sum of one million and three hundred thousand ($1,300,000) dollars, the Southwest Pacific Railroad and all the franchises, privileges, rights, titles appertaining to the same, the rolling stock, machine shop, and all the property, real and personal of every description, belonging or in any wise appertaining thereto, and the lands granted by the United States to the State of Missouri by Act of Congress approved June 10th, 1852, and by the State granted to the Pacific Railroad, for the construc-

tion of the Southwest Branch, by Act of the General Assembly of Missouri, approved December 25th, 1852.

2. The purchase money is to be paid in the following installments: One-fourth of said sum shall be payable on the execution and delivery to me of the deed of conveyance provided for in section eight of the Act to provide for the sale of certain railroads, approved February 19th, 1866, and the balance in four equal annual installments—the first installment payable in one year, the second in two years, the third in three years, and the fourth in four years after the execution and delivery of said deed, with six per cent. interest on the deferred payments, payable annually; provided that any part or the whole of said sums may be paid at maturity, or at any time before maturity, in either cash or bonds, or other liabilities of the State, or bonds guaranteed by the State, which bonds are to be taken in payment for the amount of principal and interest due on the same; and in case of payment of any installment before maturity, interest on the same shall be collected only to the day of payment of the same.

3. The Southwest Pacific Railroad and rolling stock belonging thereto shall be kept in good serviceable condition during the progress of the work to the completion of the road.

4. The work of construction shall be commenced by me, my associates or assigns, within thirty days after the delivery of the deed to me, and shall be finished to a point opposite the town of Lebanon, in Laclede County, within one year and nine months thereafter; to the town of Springfield, in Greene County, within two years and six months thereafter; and to the western line of the State in three years and six months thereafter; provided that if on examination it shall be found practicable and lawful to avoid a proposed tunnel and heavy embankment between Little Piney and the town of Lebanon, which proposed works are the ruling feature of the present location of the road, the period of completion to the points named shall be shortened so as to be as follows: to Lebanon within one year and six months, to Springfield within two years, and to the State line in three years.

5. I bind myself to expend at least five hundred thousand dollars in each and every year between the date of sale and date

fixed for the completion aforesaid, in work upon the graduation, masonry, superstructure and equipment of said extension.

6. This purchase shall be made subject to the conditions of forfeiture enumerated in the fourteenth section of the Act of the General Assembly approved February 19th, 1866, providing for the sale of certain railroads, &c.

7. For the amount of purchase money remaining unpaid, the State shall retain and have a first lien on all property and franchises purchased by me, which lien shall be evidenced by a mortgage to be executed by me, my associates and assigns in conformity with the provisions of the eighth section of said act.

8. By said purchase, I shall be deemed to have acquired all the rights, franchises, privileges and immunities granted to the purchaser by the provisions of said Act, and the act amendatory thereto, and particularly those enumerated in the ninth section of said act.

9. As purchaser of said road, franchises, etc., I, my associates and assigns shall have the right to borrow money for the completion of said road and payment of the purchase money to the State, in such amounts and denominations, on such terms and in such form as may be thought proper by myself, associates and assigns. And I, my associates and assigns, shall have the right to secure the money borrowed and the evidence thereof— whether in the shape of bonds or otherwise, by a mortgage or deed of trust or pledges of the finished or unfinished portion of the road and appurtenances and lands acquired by said purchase, without being subject in relation to such loans, bonds, mortgages and pledges, to any conditions or restrictions enumerated in the tenth section of said act of the General Assembly, providing for the sale of certain railroads, etc., approved February 19th, 1866.

10. In consideration of the premises, the State shall carry out the provisions of the eleventh section of said act, and you, gentlemen, Commissioners, are expected and requested to use your best endeavors to carry into effect the provisions of the thir-

teenth section of said act before the execution and delivery of the deed.

11. To enable me to carry out this proposal, if accepted by you, it is necessary that no time should be lost in commencing work. I, therefore, request an acceptance of or reply to my proposition within two days, reserving to myself the right to withdraw the same if not accepted within that time. In case of an acceptance of my proposal, I expect the necessary contracts and deeds to be executed within reasonable time.

(Signed)   J. C. FREMONT.

EMIL PREETORIUS, his Attorney in fact.

St. Louis, Mo., May 12th, 1866.

Commissioners' Office, S. W. P. R. R., May 12th, 1866.

The foregoing proposal is accepted by us, and is recommended for approval to his excellency the Governor of Missouri.

(Signed)   P. JOS. OSTERHAUS,
R. J. McELHANEY,
A. W. MAUPIN.

Approved.

(Signed)   THOMAS C. FLETCHER.

In testimony whereof, I, Thomas C. Fletcher, Governor of the State of Missouri, have hereunto set my hand and caused
[L.S.]   to be affixed the great seal of the State of Missouri.
Done at the city of Jefferson, this seventeenth day of May, A. D., 1866.

By the Governor.

(Signed)   FRANCIS RODMAN,
Secretary of State.

Whereas, By virtue and under authority of the fourth section
of an Act of the General Assembly of Missouri, entitled " An
" Act to provide for the sale of certain railroads and property by
" the Governor, to foreclose the State lien thereon and to secure
" an early completion of the Southwest Branch Pacific, the
" Platte Country, the St. Louis and Iron Mountain, and the Cairo
" and Fulton Railroads, of Missouri, approved February 19th,
" 1866," the undersigned Board of Commissioners did publish a
notice for at least sixty days, inviting proposals for the purchase
of the Southwest Pacific Railroad (formerly known as the Southwest Branch of the Pacific Railroad), together with the lands,
appurtenances and franchises thereto belonging ; and whereas,
on the day named in said notice, to wit, on the 9th day of May,
A. D. 1866, said Board of Commissioners proceeded to compare
the several bids and proposals by them received, and deeming
them unsatisfactory, rejected the same ; and, whereas, in pursuance of the seventh section of said act, the Governor of the State
of Missouri did in writing direct the said Commissioners, on the
10th day of May, 1866, to sell said road and all its lands, property, franchises and appurtenances at private sale ; and, whereas,
John C. Fremont, on the twelfth day of May, 1866, made a proposal in writing to said Commissioners, for the purchase of
said road at private sale, under the provisions of the seventh section of said act, a true copy of which proposal is hereto attached
and made part of this contract, except so far as the terms thereof are modified by the terms herein provided ; and, whereas, said
proposal was, on the twelfth day of May, 1866, duly accepted by
said board of Commissioners, and the sale so made was approved
by said Governor ; *Now, therefore*, this agreement, made and entered into this twenty-eighth day of May, A. D. 1866, by and between
P. Jos. Osterhaus and Robt. J. McElhaney, constituting a majority of the Board of Commissioners aforesaid, acting on behalf of
the State of Missouri, under the authority of the act aforesaid,
parties of the first part, and John C. Fremont, of the City of
New York, party of the second part, *Witnesseth : First*, that
said John C. Fremont has agreed, and by these presents does
agree to buy, and said Commissioners have agreed to sell to said
John C. Fremont, for the sum of one million and three hundred
thousand dollars ($1,300,000), the Southwest Pacific Railroad
(formerly called the Southwest Branch of the Pacific Railroad),

and all the franchises, privileges, rights, titles, choses in action, and easements appertaining to the same; the rolling stock, cars, engines, depots, machine shops, and all the property, real and personal of every description, belonging or in any wise appertaining thereto, and the lands granted by the United States to the State of Missouri, by an act of Congress entitled "An Act granting the "right of way to the State of Missouri, &c.," approved June 10, 1852, and by said State granted to the Pacific Railroad Company for the construction of the Southwest Branch of the Pacific Railroad by act of the General Assembly of Missouri, approved December 25th, 1852, and all other subsequent acts relating to said Southwest Branch Railroad and the Pacific Railroad; and generally all property, rights, titles and franchises appertaining to said Southwest Branch Railroad which have become the property of the State by operation of law, whether reduced to possession by the State or the Governor of the State, or not.

Secondly. That the purchase money is to be paid in the following installments: one-fourth of said sum shall be payable on the execution and delivery to said John C. Fremont of the formal deed of conveyance provided to be executed and delivered to the purchaser by the Governor of the State, under the provisions of the eighth section of the act of February 19th, 1866, aforesaid. The balance of said purchase money shall be paid in four equal annual installments; the first payable in one year, the second in two years, the third in three years, and the fourth in four years after the execution and delivery of said deed, with six per cent. interest on the deferred payments, payable annually; *provided*, that any part or the whole of said sums may be paid at maturity or any time before maturity, either in cash or bonds, or other liabilities of the State, or bonds guaranteed by the State, which bonds are to be taken in payment for the amount of principal and interest due on the same, and in case of payment of any installment before maturity, interest on the same shall be collected only to the day of payment thereof.

Thirdly. The Southwest Pacific Railroad and rolling stock belonging thereto shall be kept in good serviceable condition by the purchaser, or his representatives or assigns, during the progress of the work to the completion of the road.

Fourthly. The work of construction shall be commenced by said John C. Fremont, his associates or assigns, within thirty days after the delivery to him of the deed, and shall be finished to a point opposite the town of Lebanon, in Laclede County, within one year and nine months thereafter; and to the town of Springfield, in Greene County, within two years and six months; and to the western line of the State in three years and six months after the delivery of the said deed; *provided* that if upon examination it shall be found practicable and lawful to avoid a proposed tunnel and heavy embankment between the Little Piney and the town of Lebanon, which proposed works are the ruling features of the present location of the road, the change may be adopted, and the periods of completion to the points named shall be shortened so as to be as follows: to Lebanon within one year and six months, to Springfield within two years, and to the western line of the State in three years.

Fifthly. The said John C. Fremont binds himself and his associates, representatives and assigns, to expend at least five hundred thousand dollars in each and every year between the date of sale and the date fixed for the completion of the road as provided herein, in work upon the graduation, masonry, superstructures and equipment of said extension.

Sixthly. Any failure on the part of said John C. Fremont, his associates or assigns, to pay the purchase money as herein provided, and to expend the sums of money required as herein stated, for the completion of the road, or any failure to keep and perform any of the conditions of this agreement, by him or them to be kept and performed, shall work a forfeiture of said road, its franchises, rolling stock, appurtenances and other property, both real and personal, to the State of Missouri; and in case the Governor deem it advisable, he shall then proceed at once to take possession of the same, without aid of any writ or process of law; shall hold and operate the same through such agents as he may appoint therefor, until the General Assembly shall otherwise dispose of the same, for the purpose of foreclosing the State's lien or mortgage, or, at his option, may proceed to sell the same to the highest bidder, for cash or bonds of the State, at public vendue, at the east front door of the Court House in St. Louis, Missouri, first having given notice of the time, terms and place of sale, and of the property to be sold, by advertisement in one daily newspaper published in each of the cities of St. Louis, New York, Boston and Philadelphia, for three months prior to the day of sale.

Seventhly. For the amount of purchase money remaining unpaid, and for the performance of each and all of the conditions and undertakings by the said John C. Fremont and his associates or assigns, to be performed under this contract, the state shall have the first lien which said Fremont can give upon all the property and franchises purchased by said Fremont, which lien shall be evidenced by a mortgage upon said property and franchises, in due form of law, and in accordance with the terms of this contract.

Eighthly. By the purchase and deed of conveyance above mentioned, the said John C. Fremont and his representatives, associates or assigns, shall acquire all the rights, franchises, privileges and immunities granted to the purchaser by the provisions of said act authorizing this contract, and the acts amendatory thereof; and said Fremont, his associates, assigns and legal representatives, shall thereby acquire, and may at their option avail themselves of all the rights, franchises, privileges and immunities, which were had and enjoyed by the Pacific Railroad Company, for whose default said Southwest Pacific Railroad was sold, under the charter of the said Pacific Railroad Company and the laws amendatory thereof, subject, however, to the conditions and limitations therein contained, and not inconsistent with the act under which this contract is made.

Ninthly. As purchasers of said road, franchises, etc., said John C. Fremont, his associates and assigns, shall have the right to borrow money for the completion of said road and payment of the purchase money to the State, in such amounts and denominations, on such terms and form as they may deem best, without being subject to the requirements or conditions of the tenth section of said act, approved February 19th, 1866 ; *provided*, and it is hereby understood, that the lien of the state for any of the matters aforesaid is not to be waived, or in any wise impaired.

Tenthly. In consideration of the premises, the State of Missouri has agreed to carry into effect the provisions, and to perform the conditions, of the eleventh section of said act of the General Assembly, approved 19th February, 1866, under which this sale is made; and in pursuance of said provisions, the State of Missouri hereby agrees that the act approved March 2d, 1861, entitled "An Act concerning the bonds of the Pacific Railroad guaran- "teed by the State," shall remain in full force, and that the State assumes the full payment of such guaranteed bonds, not exchanged, as provided for in said act, and will hold said John C. Fremont, his associates, assigns, and legal representatives, harmless on account of said outstanding bonds, and that the Governor shall take all steps necessary and advisable to carry out the foregoing terms.

When said Fremont, his associates, assigns and legal representatives, shall have constructed and in running order twenty miles of said road, extending on their line west of Rolla, and shall exhibit satisfactory proof thereof to the Governor of the State, in order that said Fremont, his associates, and assigns, and legal representatives, may be enabled to make title to such lands as they are authorized to sell, the Governor of the State shall and will issue the necessary certificate to the Secretary of the Interior, as provided for in section five of the act of Congress entitled "An Act granting the right of way to the State of Missouri, &c.," approved June 10, 1852. And in consideration of the premises, the Commissioners will use their best endeavors to carry into effect the provisions of the thirteenth section of the act under which this contract is made, and the said John C. Fremont shall have the benefit of any action taken under the provisions of said act; and any act or proceeding in law which may be commenced by said Commissioners before a sale be completed, shall continue thereafter in their names for the benefit of said Fremont, his associates, assigns and legal representatives.

In witness whereof, the said Commissioners of the Southwest Pacific Railroad, by the majority thereof, on behalf of the State, and by virtue of the power in them vested by the acts aforesaid, and the said John C. Fremont, by his lawfully appointed attorney in fact, have hereto set their hands and seals the said twenty-eighth day of May, A. D. 1866.

(Signed)

Board of Commissioners { P. JOS. OSTERHAUS, [seal.]
Southwest Pacific Railroad, { R. J. McELHANEY. [seal.]
JOHN C. FREMONT. [seal.]
By Emil Preetorius, his Attorney in fact.

Done in duplicate.

All interlineations, erasures and alterations made before delivery hereof.

Witness: (Signed) Chester Harding, Jr.
James Taussig.

Approved June the 13th, A. D. 1866.

In testimony whereof, I have hereunto set my hand and caused the *Great Seal* of the *State of Missouri* to be affixed.

[seal.] Done at the City of Jefferson, this thirteenth day of June, A. D. 1866, of the independence of the United States the ninetieth, and of the State of Missouri the forty-sixth.

THOS. C. FLETCHER.

By the Governor,
Francis Rodman, Secretary of State.

Office of the Secretary of State, }
City of Jefferson, Missouri. }

I, Francis Rodman, Secretary of the State of Missouri, hereby certify, that the annexed pages contain a true, complete, and full copy of the proposals made and contract entered into by and between John C. Fremont and the Board of Commissioners of the Southwest Pacific Railroad, relative to the sale of the said Southwest Pacific Railroad, as appears by comparing the same with the original roll of said proposal and contract, now on file, as the law directs, in this office.

In testimony whereof, I have hereunto set my hand and [seal.] affixed my official seal. Done at office, this fourteenth day of June, A. D. eighteen hundred and sixty-six.

FRANCIS RODMAN,
Secretary of State.

```
┌─────────────┐
│ U. S. STAMP.│
│   $1.00     │
│   J. C. F.  │
│  June 4, '66.│
└─────────────┘
```

Know all men by these Presents:

That we, John C. Fremont, of the City of New York, and State of New York, and Jessie Benton Fremont, wife of said John C. Fremont, have made, constituted and appointed, and by these presents do make, constitute and appoint, James Taussig, of the City of St. Louis, and State of Missouri, our true and lawful attorney, for us and in our names, place and stead, or in the name, place and stead of either of us, to execute, acknowledge and deliver to the State of Missouri, or to the Governor of that State, or other proper officer, a mortgage on the Southwest Pacific Railroad, its franchises, lands, and property, pursuant to the act of the General Assembly of the State of Missouri, entitled "An Act to provide for the sale of certain railroads," &c., &c., approved February 19th, 1866, to secure the payment of the unpaid portion of the purchase money for said Southwest Pacific Railroad, its franchises, lands and property lately purchased by said John C. Fremont, under the authority of said act; also to secure the performance of the other undertakings, covenants and agreements mentioned and set forth in the contract of sale of said road to said Gen'l John C. Fremont, made and entered into on the 28th day of May, 1866, between the State of Missouri, by its commissioners, under said act, and said John C. Fremont, and by him or his assigns and representatives to be performed; and to execute, acknowledge and deliver any contracts, deeds, covenants or instruments relating to said purchase and sale, giving and granting unto our said attorney full power and authority to do and perform all and every act and thing whatsoever requisite and necessary to be done in and about the premises as fully to all intents and purposes as we might or could do if personally present, with full power of substitution and revocation, hereby ratifying and confirming all that our said attorney or his substitute shall lawfully do or cause to be done by virtue hereof. In witness whereof, we have hereunto set our hands and seals, the fourth day of June in the year one thousand eight hundred and sixty-six.

(Signed)   JOHN C. FREMONT.   [L.S.]
               JESSIE BENTON FREMONT. [L.S.]

The words "of said road" interlined before execution.

Sealed and delivered in the presence of
           CHAS. NETTLETON,
           A. NAUMANN.

STATE OF NEW YORK, } ss.
CITY AND COUNTY OF NEW YORK,

I, Charles Nettleton, a Commissioner for Missouri in the State and City of New York, do hereby certify that on this fourth day of June, A. D. one thousand eight hundred and sixty-six, personally came before me John C. Fremont and Jessie Benton Fremont, his wife, who are personally known to me to be the same persons described in and whose names are subscribed to the within and foregoing power of attorney as parties thereto, and severally acknowledged the same to be their act and deed for the uses and purposes therein mentioned, and the said Jessie Benton Fremont, wife of the said John C. Fremont, having been by me first made acquainted with the contents of said power of attorney, acknowledged on an examination apart from her husband that she executed the same, and thereby relinquished and authorized the relinquishment of her dower in the real estate therein mentioned, freely and without compulsion or undue influence of her husband. In witness whereof, I have hereunto set my hand and affixed my official seal on this 4th day of June, A. D. 1866.

(Signed)   CHARLES NETTLETON,
[SEAL.]   Commissioner for Missouri, in New York.

STATE OF MISSOURI, } ss.
COUNTY OF ST. LOUIS,

I, the undersigned, Recorder for said County, certify that the foregoing instrument of writing was filed for record in my office June 15th, 1866, and is truly recorded in Book 320, page 171.

Witness my hand and official seal, date aforesaid.

[SEAL.]   JULIUS CONRAD, Recorder.

{ Not subject to Stamp Duty. W. TAUSSIG. }

THIS DEED made and entered into this fourteenth day of June, in the year of our Lord one thousand eight hundred and sixty-six, by and between the State of Missouri, party of the first part, and John C. Fremont, of the city of New-York, in the State of New-York, party of the second part, *witnesseth*, that the said State of Missouri, party of the first part, acting through Thomas C. Fletcher, Governor of the State, who executes these presents by virtue and under authority of the power vested in him by the provisions of the eighth section of an act of the General Assembly of the State of Missouri, entitled "An act to provide for the sale of certain railroads and property, &c.," approved February 19th, 1866, in consideration of the sum of one million and three hundred thousand dollars, paid to the said party of the first part by the said party of the second part, the receipt whereof is hereby acknowledged, and in further consideration and pursuance of the terms of a duplicate contract entered into by the Board of Commissioners for the Southwest Pacific Railroad with said party of the second part, on the twenty-eighth day of May, A. D. 1866, approved by the Governor and filed in the office of the Secretary of State as provided by law, has granted, bargained, sold, conveyed, confirmed, assigned and transferred, and by these presents does grant, bargain, sell, convey, confirm, assign and transfer unto the said John C. Fremont the Southwest Pacific Railroad, formerly known as the Southwest Branch of the Pacific Railroad, and all the franchises, privileges, rights, choses in action and easements appertaining to the same; the rolling stock, cars, engines, depots, machine-shops, tanks and all property real and personal of every description belonging or in anywise appertaining thereto, and also the lands granted by the United States to the State of Missouri by an act of Congress, entitled "An act granting the right of way "to the State of Missouri and a portion of the public lands, &c.," approved June 10th, 1852, and by the State of Missouri granted to the Pacific Railroad by an act of the General Assembly of the State of Missouri, entitled "An act to accept a grant of land made to the State of Missouri," approved December 25th, 1852, and all other subsequent acts of said General Assembly relating to said Southwest Branch Railroad and Pacific Railroad, and generally all property, rights, titles and franchises appertaining to said Southwest Branch Railroad and Pacific Railroad which have become the property of the State by operation of law, whether reduced to possession by the State, or the Governor of the State, or not. *To have and to hold* the said premises and appurtenances unto the said party of the second part, his heirs and assigns forever. And the State of Missouri, party of the first part, by these presents covenants to and with the said party of the second part, his heirs, executors, administrators and assigns, that the said party of the first part shall and will well and truly perform the conditions and stipulations of the eleventh section of said act of the General Assembly, approved February 19th, 1866; and that the said party of the first part shall and will well and truly perform and fulfil the conditions by her assumed to be performed by the terms of the contract of sale hereinbefore referred to. And it is hereby further covenanted and agreed by and between the parties hereto that the said John C. Fremont, his heirs, assigns or legal representatives may at their option avail themselves of all the rights, franchises, privileges and immunities which were had and enjoyed by the Pacific Railroad, for whose default said Southwest Pacific Railroad was sold, under the charter of said Pacific Railroad and the laws amendatory and supplementary thereto, subject, however, to the conditions and limitations therein contained. *In testimony whereof,* I, Thos. C. Fletcher, Governor of the State of Missouri, have hereunto set my hand and caused the great seal of the State of Missouri to be affixed hereto.

Done at the city of Jefferson, this 14th day of June, A. D., 1866. of the independence of the United States the ninetieth, and of the State of Missouri the forty-sixth.

THOMAS C. FLETCHER. [L. S.]

[STATE SEAL.]   By the Governor.

FRANCIS RODMAN,
Secretary of State.

STATE OF MISSOURI, *ss.*

Be it remembered, that Thomas C. Fletcher, who is personally known to the undersigned, Clerk of the Supreme Court within

and for the State aforesaid, to be the same person whose name is
subscribed to the foregoing deed as party thereto, this day appeared before me and acknowledged that he executed and delivered the same as the act and deed of the State of Missouri, by
and through him, the said Thomas C. Fletcher, as Governor of
said State, for the uses and purposes therein contained.

In testimony whereof, I hereto set my hand and affix the seal
of our said Supreme Court, at office in the city of Jeffer-
[L.S.]   son, this fourteenth day of June, A. D. eighteen hundred and sixty-six.

    :   N. C. BURCH, Clerk.

Filed and recorded June 15th, 1866.

              JULIUS CONRAD, Recorder.

> Not subject to Stamp Duty.
> WM. TAUSSIG,
> Collector of Internal Revenue.

STATE OF MISSOURI, }
COUNTY OF ST. LOUIS, } ss.

I, the undersigned, Recorder for said County, certify that the
foregoing instrument of writing was filed for record in my office
June 15th, 1866, and is truly recorded in book 320, page 170.

Witness my hand and official seal, date aforesaid.

[L.S.]   JULIUS CONRAD, Recorder.

STATE OF MISSOURI, }
COUNTY OF ST. LOUIS, } ss.

I, the undersigned, Recorder for the said county, certify the
foregoing to be a true and complete copy of an instrument of
writing from the State of Missouri to John C. Fremont, and of
the certificate of acknowledgment, and of the date of filing and
recording thereof, as fully as the same remains of record in my
office, in book 320, page 170.

Witness my hand and official seal, this the 19th day of
June, 1866.

[L.S.]   JULIUS CONRAD,
                         Recorder.

56

U. S. STAMP.

$1000

J. C. F.

June 14, '66.

Know all men by these Presents: That we, John C. Fremont
and Jessie Benton Fremont, his wife, both of the City of New
York, in the State of New York, acting by and through James
Taussig, of St. Louis, Missouri, our duly authorized attorney, in
consideration of the sum of one dollar to us paid by Thomas C.
Fletcher, Governor of the State of Missouri, on behalf of said
State, the receipt whereof we do hereby acknowledge, do give,
grant, sell, transfer and assign unto the State of Missouri, the
Southwest Pacific Railroad (formerly known as the Southwest
Branch of the Pacific Railroad), and all the franchises, privileges,
choses in action and easements appertaining to the same; the
rolling stock, cars, engines, depots, machine shops, tanks and all
the property, real and personal of every description, belonging
or in any wise appertaining thereto, and also all the lands granted by the United States to the State of Missouri, by an act of
Congress, entitled "An Act granting the right of way to the
"State of Missouri, etc.," approved June 10th, 1852, and by the
State granted to said John C. Fremont, by deed of even date
herewith, and generally all property, rights, titles and franchises
appertaining to said Southwest Branch Railroad, which were acquired by said John C. Fremont by the formal deed of conveyance of the State of Missouri to him, of even date herewith, and
hereinafter particularly referred to; *Provided, nevertheless,* and
this conveyance is made upon the express condition that whereas,
on the twenty-eighth day of May, A. D. eighteen hundred and
sixty-six, the Board of Commissioners of the Southwest Pacific
Railroad did, on behalf of the State of Missouri, enter into a duplicate contract with said John C. Fremont, for the sale of the
said Southwest Pacific Railroad, and all its appurtenances, which
contract was afterwards, to wit, on the thirteenth day of June,
A. D. 1866, approved by the Governor, and one copy whereof was
afterwards filed in the office of the Secretary of State, all of
which proceedings were had in pursuance of the provisions of
the act of the General Assembly of Missouri entitled "An Act
"to provide for the sale of certain railroads and property by the

"Governor, &c.," approved February 19th, 1866; and whereas, in pursuance of the condition of said contract, and the provisions of said act, the Governor of the State of Missouri has executed and delivered to said John C. Fremont a formal deed of convey- ance of the premises hereinbefore described; and whereas it is provided in said contract, a copy whereof, duly certified by the Secretary of State, is hereto attached, and made part and parcel of this deed; that in consideration of the execution and delivery of said deed, and of the other agreements and obligations entered into by the State in said contract, he, the said John C. Fremont, should secure the portion of the purchase money remaining un- paid, to wit: the sum of *nine hundred and seventy-five thousand* dollars, and the due performance of the obligations by him as- sumed in said contract, by a mortgage on the property so to him conveyed; *Now, therefore,* if the said John C. Fremont, his assigns, legal representatives or successors, shall well and truly pay to the State of Missouri the installments of the purchase money men- tioned in said contract and remaining unpaid, at or before the maturity thereof, with interest, according to the terms of said contract, and if the said John C. Fremont, his assigns, successors or legal representatives, shall well and truly perform each and all of the conditions and undertakings to be by him performed under said contract, then this deed shall be absolutely void to all intents and purposes, and the lien thereby created shall be re- leased at the cost of the said Fremont or his legal representatives, by a deed of release duly executed on behalf and in the name of the State, by the Governor thereof for the time being. But if the said John C. Fremont, his assigns, successors, or legal represen- tatives, shall fail to make any of the payments as in said contract provided, or shall fail to perform any of the conditions or under- takings of said contract by him to be performed, then and in such case this deed shall remain in force, and the Governor of the State for the time being may, if in his opinion it would be to the interest of the State, proceed to sell the Railroad, its appurtenances and franchises, as herein conveyed, for cash or bonds of the State, at public vendue, at the east front door of the Court House in St. Louis, Missouri, first having given no- tice of the time, terms and place of said sale, and of the property to be sold, by advertisement in one daily newspaper published in each of the cities of St. Louis, New York, Boston, and Philadelphia, for three months prior to the day of sale; and upon such sale the Governor of the State shall execute and deliver to the purchaser or purchasers of said Railroad a deed of conveyance of the property sold, and out of the proceeds of such sale the Governor shall pay over to the Treasurer of the State, or such other person as the General Assembly may designate, whatever of the debt herein secured may then remain unpaid, and the balance, if any, shall be paid over to said John C. Fremont or his legal representatives. And it is hereby covenanted and agreed, that until default of the payment of the said sums or interest herein secured, or other default as herein provided, the said mortgagee shall have no right to enter and take possession of the premises. And it is further covenanted and agreed, by and between the parties hereto, that nothing herein contained shall be so construed as to curtail, diminish or destroy the right of the said John C. Fremont, his assigns, legal representatives or successors, to borrow money for the completion of said Southwest Pacific Railroad and payment of the purchase money to the State, in such amounts and denominations, on such terms and in such form as may be thought proper by him, his assigns or successors; and to secure the money so borrowed and the evidence thereof, whether in the shape of bonds or otherwise, by mortgage or deeds of trust, or pledges of the finished or unfinished portion of the road and appurtenances and lands acquired by said purchase, without being subject in relation to such loans, bonds, mortgages, deeds of trust and pledges to any conditions or restrictions enumerated in the tenth section of the said act of the General Assembly, approved February 19th, 1866, *provided* that such loans, bonds, mortgages, deeds of trust and pledges shall not in anywise impair the lien of the State created by these presents.

In testimony whereof, the said John C. Fremont and Jessie Benton Fremont have hereunto set their hands and affixed their seals, this fourteenth day of June, A. D. 1866.

(Signed)

JOHN C. FREMONT,   [SEAL.]
By JAMES TAUSSIG, his attorney in fact.

JESSIE BENTON FREMONT, [SEAL.]
By JAMES TAUSSIG, her attorney in fact.

59

STATE OF MISSOURI, *ss.*

Be it remembered, that on this fourteenth day of June, A. D. 1866, before me, the undersigned, Clerk of the Supreme Court of the State aforesaid, appeared James Taussig, who is personally known to me to be the same person whose name is subscribed to the foregoing instrument of writing as party thereto, and acknowledged the same to be the act and deed of John C. Fremont and Jessie Benton Fremont by and through the said James Taussig, their attorney in fact, for the uses and purposes therein mentioned, and the said James Taussig acknowledged said instrument to be his act and deed as the attorney in fact of John C. Fremont and Jessie Benton Fremont, for the uses and purposes therein mentioned, and the said James Taussig further acknowledged that by virtue and authority of the power of attorney to him executed by the said John C. Fremont and Jessie Benton Fremont, he relinquishes the dower of said Jessie Benton Fremont in the real estate in said instrument described and conveyed, and that she, the said Jessie Benton Fremont, through her said attorney, relinquishes her dower in the real estate in said instrument described, and conveys freely and voluntarily and without compulsion or undue influence on the part of her said husband.

In testimony whereof, I hereto set my hand and affixed the seal of our said Supreme Court, at office in the City of [L.S.] Jefferson, this fourteenth day of June, A. D. 1866.

(Signed)　　　　　　　　N. C. BURCH,
　　　　　　　　　　Clerk Supreme Court of Missouri.

Filed and recorded June 15th, 1866.
　　　　　　　　JULIUS CONRAD, Recorder.

STATE OF MISSOURI, } *ss.*
COUNTY OF ST. LOUIS,

I, the undersigned, Recorder for said county, certify the foregoing to be a true and complete copy of an instrument of writing from John C. Fremont to the State of Missouri, and of the certificate of acknowledgment and of the date of filing and recording thereof as fully as the same remains of record in my office, in book 320, page 171.

Witness my hand and official seal, this the 19th day of June, 1866.
[L.S.]　　　　　　(Signed)　　JULIUS CONRAD, Recorder.

DEED.

J. C. Fremont and wife to the Southwest Pacific Railroad Company.

THIS INDENTURE, made the twelfth day of September, in the year of our Lord one thousand eight hundred and sixty-six, *Between* John C. Fremont, and Jessie Benton Fremont, his wife, of the city, county and state of New York, of the first part, and the Southwest Pacific Railroad Company, a corporation created under and by virtue of an act of the General Assembly of the state of Missouri, entitled "An Act authorizing the incorporation of the purchaser or purchasers of any Railroad, &c.," "approved March 20th, 1866," party of the second part, witnesseth, that the said parties of the first part, for and in consideration of the sum of one million three hundred thousand dollars, lawful money of the United States of America, to them in hand paid by the said party of the second part, at or before the ensealing and delivery of these presents, the receipt whereof is hereby acknowledged, hath granted, bargained, sold, aliened, remised, released, conveyed and confirmed, and by these presents doth grant, bargain, sell, alien, remise, release, convey and confirm unto the said party of the second part and to its successors and assigns forever, all the Southwest Pacific Railroad formerly known as the Southwest Branch of the Pacific Railroad, and all the franchises, privileges, rights, choses in action and easements appertaining to the same, the rolling stock, cars, engines, depots, machine shops, tanks, and all property, real and personal, of every description, belonging or in anywise appertaining thereto, and also all the land granted by the United States to the said state of Missouri to aid in the construction of said road, by an act of Congress entitled "An Act granting the right of way to the state of Missouri and a portion of the public lands, &c.," approved June 10th, 1852, and which by the said state of Missouri were granted to the said John C. Fremont, one of said parties of the first part, by deed dated June 14th, 1866, and duly recorded in the office of the recorder of St.

Louis county, state of Missouri, in book 321, p. 170, on 15th June, 1866, and generally all property, rights, titles and franchises appertaining to said Southwest Branch Railroad which were so acquired by the said Fremont as aforesaid, subject nevertheless to a certain Indenture of Mortgage, bearing date the 14th day of June, 1866, made by the said parties hereto of the first part to the state of Missouri, to secure the sum of nine hundred and seventy-five thousand dollars, and recorded in the office of the recorder of St. Louis county, Missouri, in book 320, p. 171, which mortgage the said party of the second part hereby assumes and agrees to pay as part of the consideration money hereof, together with all and singular the tenements, hereditaments, and appurtenances thereunto belonging or in any wise appertaining, and the reversion and reversions, remainder and remainders, rents, issues and profits thereof; and also all the estate, right, title, interest, dower and right of dower, property, possession, claim and demand whatsoever, as well in law as in equity, of the said parties of the first part, of, in, or to the above-described premises, and every part and parcel thereof, with the appurtenances. To have and hold all and singular the above-mentioned and described premises, together with the appurtenances, the said party of the second part, its successors or assigns forever.

In witness whereof, the said parties of the first part have hereunto set their hands and seals, the day and year first above written.

J. C. FREMONT, [L.S.]

JESSIE BENTON FREMONT. [L.S.]

Sealed and delivered } CHARLES NETTLETON,
in the presence of } SUSAN C. HASKELL.

STATE OF NEW YORK, }
CITY AND COUNTY OF NEW YORK, } ss.

I, Charles Nettleton, Commissioner of Missouri in New York, do hereby certify that on this twelfth day of September, A. D. one thousand eight hundred and sixty-six, came before me John C. Fremont and Jessie Benton Fremont, his wife, who are personally known to me to be the same persons whose names are subscribed to the within indenture as parties thereto, and severally acknowledged the same to be their act and deed for the purposes therein mentioned, and the said Jessie Benton Fremont, wife of the said John C. Fremont, having been by me first made acquainted with the contents of said indenture, acknowledged on an examination apart from her husband that she executed the same, and relinquishes her dower in the real estate therein mentioned freely and without compulsion or undue influence of her husband. In testimony whereof, I have hereto set my hand and affixed my official seal the day and year aforesaid.

(Signed)   CHARLES NETTLETON,

[SEAL.]   Commissioner for Missouri in New York.

```
$1,300
Int. Rev.
Stamp
Cancelled.
```

[This deed is duly recorded in the several counties of Missouri through which the route of the road runs or in which the lands lie.]

MORTGAGE

OF THE

SOUTHWEST PACIFIC RAILROAD COMPANY,

TO

JOHN P. YELVERTON AND CHARLES H. WARD.

THIS INDENTURE OF MORTGAGE, made this fifteenth day of September, in the year of our Lord eighteen hundred and sixty-six, *Between* THE SOUTHWEST PACIFIC RAILROAD COMPANY, a corporation created under and by virtue of an act of the General Assembly of Missouri, entitled " An act authorizing the incorporation of the purchaser or purchasers of any railroad," &c., approved March 20th, 1866, of the first part, and John P. Yelverton and Charles H. Ward, of the City of New York, of the second part

Witnesseth, That whereas the said parties of the first part were incorporated as aforesaid, for the purpose of purchasing from John C. Fremont, of New York, and taking possession of the said Southwest Pacific Railroad (formerly known as the Southwest Branch of the Pacific Railroad), theretofore sold to said Fremont by the State of Missouri, and of the property, real and personal, choses in action, franchises, rights and privileges to the said Fremont conveyed by the said State of Missouri in pursuance of such sale, and to enable the said Fremont and his associates to complete, furnish, equip, operate, manage, and control such road, and the property, franchises and appurtenances thereto belonging, or in anywise appertaining.

AND WHEREAS, the said John C. Fremont and Jessie Benton Fremont his wife, did, by deed bearing date the twelfth day of

September, A. D. 1866, and duly recorded, convey to the said parties of the first part, their successors and assigns, the said road, and all the franchises, privileges, choses in action and easements appertaining to the same, the rolling stock, cars, engines, depots, machine shops, tanks and all the property, real and personal, of every description belonging or in anywise appertaining to said road, and also all the lands granted by the United States to the State of Missouri to aid in the construction of said road, by an act of Congress, entitled "An act granting the right of way to the State of Missouri," &c., approved June 10th, 1852; and by said State granted to said Fremont, by deed dated June 14th, 1866, and duly recorded, and generally all property, rights, titles and franchises appertaining to said Southwest Branch Railroad which were so acquired by the said Fremont as aforesaid.

AND WHEREAS, in and by the contract of sale of the said Southwest Pacific Railroad and its appurtenances, made in pursuance of an act of the General Assembly of Missouri, entitled "An act to provide for the sale of certain railroads and property by the Governor," &c., approved February 19th, 1866, between the Board of Commissioners of said road on behalf of the State of Missouri, and the said Fremont (which contract bears date the 21st day of May, 1866, and is filed in the office of the Secretary of State of Missouri), the said Fremont, his associates and assigns, are authorized to borrow money for the completion of said road, and payment of the purchase money to the State, in such amounts and denominations, on such terms and in such form, as they may deem best, without being subject to the requirements or conditions of the tenth section of said act.

AND WHEREAS the said parties of the first part, for the purposes aforesaid, propose to make and issue their bonds or obligations in pursuance of such contract, and of their legal rights, to the extent of seven millions two hundred and fifty thousand dollars, in the manner hereinafter mentioned, and thereby to become indebted to divers persons, bodies politic or corporate who shall become holders thereof; each of such bonds to bear date on the fifteenth day of September, A. D. 1866, to be for the sum of one thousand dollars, or of five hundred dollars each, and to be payable on the fifteenth day of September, A. D. 1886, and interest on each of said bonds at and after the rate of seven per centum

per annum, to be payable on the successive first days of July
and January in every year until said principal sums named in
said bonds respectively, shall be severally paid, and the principal
as well as interest of all said bonds to be payable in the city of
New York.

Now, THEREFORE, THIS INDENTURE WITNESSETH, that the said
parties of the first part, for the purpose of securing the payment
of the sums of money mentioned in said bonds or obligations,
and each of them, with the interest thereon, according to the
true intent and meaning thereof, and also for and in consideration
of the sum of one dollar in hand paid by said parties of the
second part, the receipt whereof is hereby acknowledged, have
granted, bargained, sold, remised, released, conveyed and confirmed, and by these presents do grant, bargain, sell, remise, release, convey and confirm unto the said parties hereto of the
second part, and the survivor of them, and to their successors in
said trust, the Southwest Pacific Railroad (formerly known as
the Southwest Branch of the Pacific Railroad), including all and
singular the several pieces or parcels of land, being the roadway,
stations and depots of said road, as now completed to Rolla, in
the county of Phelps, and all and singular the roadway, stations
and depots of said road to be completed from Rolla aforesaid to
a point in the western boundary of the State of Missouri south of
the Osage river, a further distance of about two hundred miles,
and all the franchises, privileges, choses in action, and easements
appertaining to the same, the rolling stock, cars, engines, depots,
machine shops, tanks and all other personal property of every
description, belonging or in anywise appertaining thereto.

AND ALSO, six hundred and eighty-eight thousand acres of
land, situate, lying and being in the State of Missouri, adjoining
and adjacent to the uncompleted portion of said road, parts and
parcels of the lands which were granted by the said act of Congress to the State of Missouri, to aid in the construction of said
road as aforesaid, which six hundred and eighty-eight thousand
acres of land constitute two-thirds of the land so granted by the
said act of Congress, and now unsold, and are to be selected by
the parties to this indenture of the first part, and specially set
aside and appropriated to the purposes of this mortgage, and
proper schedules and lists thereof prepared, approved and con-

firmed, under the corporate seal of the parties of the first part, to be deposited with the said parties of the second part, so as to give to the same the effect of a particular and detailed description of each separate piece or parcel of land set forth in this indenture; together with all and singular the emoluments, income and advantages, tenements, hereditaments and appurtenances thereunto belonging or in anywise appertaining, and the reversion and reversions, remainder and remainders, rents, issues and profits thereof, and also all the estate, right, title and interest, property, possession, claim and demand whatsoever, at law and in equity, of the said parties of the first part of, in and to the same, and each and every part and parcel thereof, with the appurtenances. To have and to hold, all and singular the lands, premises and property hereby granted, or intended so to be, and each and every part and parcel thereof, with the appurtenances, unto the said parties of the second part, and the survivor of them and their successors in said trust, as joint tenants, and not as tenants in common, for the uses and purposes in this indenture set forth and declared, subject to the provisions and requirements of the before mentioned act of Congress, and to the several acts of the General Assembly of Missouri relating to the same, and subject also to the possession, control and management of the directors of the said parties of the first part, so long as said bonds or obligations shall remain unforfeited by the proper performance of all the stipulations thereof: *Provided always*, and these presents are upon the express condition that if the said parties of the first part shall well and truly pay or cause to be paid to the holders of said bonds or obligations, and every of them, the principal sums of money therein mentioned according to the true intent and meaning of these presents, that then and from thenceforth this indenture and the estate hereby granted shall cease, determine and be utterly void.

AND THIS INDENTURE FURTHER WITNESSETH, that these presents and the said bonds or obligations are made, executed and delivered upon the terms, conditions and agreements following; that is to say:

First.—That the actual possession, use, management and control of the said Railroad, with all the appurtenances thereto belonging, shall be and remain with the parties of the first part, so long as the said bonds or obligations shall remain without default or forfeiture, and the said parties of the first part shall perform and keep the stipulations thereof.

Second.—That in case any further grants of land in said State shall be made by any act or resolve of the United States, or of the said State of Missouri, to, or shall be otherwise acquired by, the said parties of the first part, two-thirds of the same are, by the said parties of the first part, to be conveyed to the said parties of the second part or their successors in said Trust, to be held in mortgage and trust, in the same manner and for the same purposes as the other lands which are embraced by this Indenture, and the remaining third of such lands are to be held by the said parties of the first part, and appropriated by them to the purposes mentioned in the seventh article of this Indenture, as hereinafter set forth.

Third.—That of the bonds to be issued for the purpose aforesaid, two millions thereof, and no more, shall be issued for the portion of the Road already completed to Rolla aforesaid, and the further issue thereof is restricted to twenty-five thousand dollars for each mile of Road beyond Rolla, as and after each mile shall be completed; and each of said bonds shall be countersigned by said parties of the second part.

Fourth.—That the six hundred and eighty-eight thousand acres granted as aforesaid shall be carefully valued and appraised by the said parties of the first part, their officers and agents, and the relative value of each piece or parcel of land established for the purpose of division and allotment thereof, into seven classes of the following number of acres and valuations, that is to say:

1st Class. Consisting of lands of developed lead mines, 640 acres, minimum valuation $500 per acre............................... $320,000

2d Class. Lands of lead mines not fully developed, but 1st class, 1,920 acres, minimum valuation $300 per acre.................... 576,000

3d Class. Mineral lands of special value, containing iron, coal, copper and lead, 25,000 acres, minimum valuation $50 per acre......... 1,250,000

4th Class. 1st class agricultural lands situated near towns and stations, 12,800 acres, minimum valuation $20 per acre.................. 256,000

5th Class. Superior timber and agricultural lands from peculiarity of location on line of Road, 202,306 acres, minimum valuation $15 per acre... 3,034,590

6th Class. Superior agricultural and timber lands, 224,000 acres, minimum valuation $8 per acre................................. 1,792,000

7th Class. Good agricultural and timber lands, 221,334 acres, minimum valuation $5 per acre.. 1,106,670

Forming an aggregate of 688,000 acres of............. $8,335,260

All of which the said parties of the first part, with as little delay as practicable, shall certify and declare to the said parties of the second part, by proper lists and schedules under seal, with such description as shall enable the parties of the second part to ascertain and establish the precise location, position and boundaries of each and every piece or parcel of said lands, and the class to which the same belongs, and the price or sum for which the same may be sold or conveyed, which price or sum may be varied and changed from time to time, at the pleasure of said parties of the first part. *Provided*, however, that the selling price of any piece or parcel of land shall in no case be less than the minimum valuation of the same hereinbefore given, and of the class to which it is allotted, until the aggregate sum actually realized and received in money, evidences of debt, or by the surrender of the said bonds or obligations as hereinafter provided, shall amount to the aggregate valuation of any of the classes above set forth and declared, when the said parties of the first part may instruct and empower the said parties of the second part to sell and convey any remaining pieces or parcels of land of said class, at such price as they may deem proper, even below the minimum valuation of the class, but not to alter or change the mode of selling, or the appropriation of the proceeds and receipts from such sales.

Fifth.—That the parties of the first part shall be at all times at liberty to contract for the sale of any of the divisions or parcels of said lands, at a price not less than that fixed in the valuations aforesaid, and to contract to receive payment therefor in cash, or with the written consent of the said parties of the second part may give credit on said sales, and upon the payment of such purchase money to said parties of the second part, said parties of the second part shall, by proper deeds or instruments by them executed, join in a release and conveyance of such parcel or parcels of land to the purchasers thereof, and when and so often as from the net proceeds of sales of said lands, after deducting all charges connected with the execution of said trust, there shall remain in the hands of said parties of the second part a sum equal to forty thousand dollars, said parties of the second part shall apply the same to the payment and discharge of the said bonds, secured hereby in manner following, that is to say: The said parties of the second part shall give sixty days' notice, by

publication in one or more newspapers printed in Missouri and
in the city of New York, of their readiness to redeem said bonds
at the lowest rates below, and not exceeding five per cent. above
the par value thereof and interest due thereon, at which the
holders of said bonds may offer to sell the same, and all bonds
that may be thus offered for redemption, shall be classified by the
said parties of the second part, and shall be paid and discharged
by them in the order of the lowest rates, within the limits aforesaid, at which they may be so offered, to the extent of the sum
in the hands of the said parties of the second part, and in case of
insufficiency of funds to pay and discharge all the bonds of the
same class offered for redemption, the said parties of the second
part shall determine by lot the bonds of such class which shall
be entitled to be so paid and discharged; and in the event that
no bonds shall be offered for redemption within the limits aforesaid, or not a sufficient amount thereof, to absorb the sum in the
hands of the said parties of the second part, then such sum or so
much thereof as shall not have been appropriated in the manner
aforesaid, shall, at the option of the said parties of the first part,
be payable to the said parties of the first part, to be used by
them in the construction of said Road, upon their surrendering
to the said parties of the second part, to be cancelled, an equal
amount of said bonds unissued, at the par value thereof, provided,
however, that by the terms of this mortgage, the said parties of
the first part shall have the right at that time to issue such bonds;
and in case the said sum of forty thousand dollars shall not be
appropriated in any of the ways above provided for, then such
sum or so much thereof as may not have been so appropriated
shall be invested by said parties of the second part in United
States bonds and securities, which, with the income thereof, may
be applied from time to time to the redemption of said bonds, in
the manner and within the limits aforesaid, or such securities
may be retained by the said parties of the second part, and with
the income thereof accumulated to form a sinking fund for the
payment of said bonds, when they shall become due and payable.

Sixth.—That the holders of any of the bonds hereby secured,
shall have the right at any time to receive in payment thereof at
par and interest any of said parcels of land, except the mineral
lands, at the valuation so fixed as aforesaid, at schedule rates at
time of such payment, provided the same shall not have been

previously sold or contracted to be sold, and provided also that the land so taken in payment for said bonds, shall not, in any instance, be in quantity less or other than the lots into which said lands have been divided for sale as aforesaid, and any excess in value of lands thus taken in payment, beyond such bonds and interest, shall be paid by the holders thereof in cash, to said parties of the second part, and in all such cases of the payment of any of said bonds by lands as aforesaid, said parties of the second part shall and may as well in the names of the parties of the first part as in their own names, execute and acknowledge and deliver proper deeds of release or conveyances of the lands so taken in payment as aforesaid, and all bonds received in payment for said lands or otherwise as aforesaid, shall be by said parties of the second part forthwith cancelled, the corporate seal of the parties of the first part taken therefrom, and the same be filed and preserved by said parties of the second part.

Seventh.—That three hundred and forty-four thousand acres of land, parts and parcels of the lands which were granted by the said act of Congress to the State of Missouri, to aid in the construction of said road, being one-third of the lands conveyed by said State to the said Fremont, and by said Fremont to said parties of the first part as aforesaid, and which are not included in this mortgage, shall be held and set apart by the said parties of the first part, for purposes of sale from time to time, and the proceeds of such sales shall be appropriated, in case of deficiency from other sources, to the payment of interest of said bonds and to the maintaining and operating of said road, or to the construction thereof, as the exigencies of the business of said parties of the first part may require, and if not so appropriated, the proceeds of such sales or the balance thereof after such appropriation, if any, shall go to and form part of the sinking fund for the redemption of said bonds hereinbefore provided for.

And this Indenture further witnesseth, that said parties of the first part do covenant and agree to pay to the holders of said bonds respectively, the said principal sums of money therein respectively mentioned, together with the interest as stipulated therein; and that if default shall be made in the payment of the interest of said bonds or either of them, payment thereof being duly demanded, and said default shall continue for the period of six months, or if default shall be made in the payment of the principal of said bonds or obligations, that then and from thence-

forth it shall and may be lawful for the said parties of the second
part to enter into and upon, and take possession of all and
singular the said Railroad, and all the property included or
intended to be included in this mortgage, and also all the engines,
tenders, cars, carriages, tools, machinery, and materials in any
way belonging or appertaining to said road then owned by the
said parties of the first part, in the same manner as if the same
had actually been included in and held by this Indenture of
Mortgage, and that the said parties of the second part shall, and
may by themselves, their officers and agents, take, receive, and
collect the income and profits of said railroad, first applying the
same to the payment and discharge of all the current expenses
of said railroad, and its needful repairs, and then to the payment
of the interest and principal of said bonds or obligations in such
manner as they may deem proper. And further, that the said
parties of the second part having entered into full possession of
the said railroad and all the equipments thereto belonging, as
above provided, may proceed to dispose of the same, and all and
singular the lands hereinbefore particularly set forth and described, remaining unsold at the time of such entry, if any there be,
and also each and every piece or parcel of land and premises,
parts and parcels of the lands so granted to the State of Missouri
by the said act of Congress, to aid in the construction of said
road, and which have not been and are not intended to be included in this mortgage, which may then remain unsold, in the
same manner as if said lands had been included in these presents
and mortgaged for the purposes herein set forth and declared,
and may make such sale of the said premises, each and every of
them, and all benefit and equity of redemption of the said parties
of the first part therein, at public auction, after giving public
notice of the time and place of such sale, by advertising the
same in one or more newspapers printed in the State of Missouri
and in the city of New York, at least six months before the time
fixed for such sale; and the said parties of the second part, as the
attorneys of said parties of the first part, are hereby authorized,
constituted and appointed to make and deliver to the purchaser
or purchasers, good and sufficient deed or deeds of conveyance
in the law for the same, in fee simple, and good and sufficient
transfers and assignments of such personal property; and out of
the money arising from such sale and sales, to retain the principal
and interest which shall then be due on said bonds or obligations,

for the benefit of the holders thereof, together with the costs and charges of advertisement and sale of said premises, rendering the overplus of the purchase money, if any, unto the said parties of the first part, their successors or assigns, which sale shall forever be a perpetual bar against the said parties of the first part, their successors and assigns, and all other persons claiming or to claim the premises, or any part thereof, by, from, or under them or either of them.

And it is hereby mutually agreed by and between the parties to these presents, that the said parties of the second part, and their successors in said trust, their heirs, executors, or administrators, shall not be answerable for the acts, defaults, or omissions of each other, and that each shall be responsible for gross negligence and willful default only.

And it is further agreed, by and between the said parties of the second part, that whenever a vacancy among said parties of the second part or their successors shall occur by death, resignation, or inability to discharge the duties of said trust, the remaining Trustee shall immediately proceed and make an appointment of a successor from among the holders of said bonds or obligations, by endorsing such appointment in writing upon this Indenture, and the person so appointed shall endorse his acceptance of such appointment upon the Indenture, and thereupon such person shall become Trustee with the surviving or remaining party of the second part, and the said surviving or remaining party of the second part shall, by appropriate instruments, vest in the party so appointed, the necessary legal estate and interest to enable him to execute said trust, and in case said vacancy shall not be filled within thirty days from the occurrence thereof, by said remaining Trustee as aforesaid, or in case of the death or resignation of both of said Trustees, then and thereupon such vacancy or vacancies may be filled by the parties of the first part, from among the holders of said bonds, in the manner aforesaid, such bondholder or bondholders so chosen as last aforesaid to fill such vacancy or vacancies, to be each the *bona fide* owner of not less than twenty thousand dollars of said bonds, at par value thereof.

All such resignations so made as aforesaid shall be in writing endorsed hereon, and signed by the party so resigning, and any such disability certified hereon by the remaining Trustee and confirmed by the vote of the Directors of the parties of the first part, shall be taken and deemed to be conclusive in the premises.

73

And it is further agreed by said parties of the first part, that they, their successors, and all and every person or persons whomsoever legally or equitably deriving any estate, right, title or interest of, in, or to the premises hereinbefore granted by, from, under or in trust for them, shall and will, at any time or times hereafter, upon the reasonable request and at the proper costs and charges in the law of the said parties of the second part, their heirs and assigns, make, do and execute, and cause to be made, done and executed, all and every such further and other reasonable acts, conveyances and assurances in the law for the better and more effectually vesting and confirming the premises hereby granted or intended so to be, in and to the said parties of the second part, their heirs and assigns forever, as by the said parties of the second part, their heirs or assigns, or their counsel learned in the law, shall be reasonably desired, advised or required.

And it is further agreed, that the parties of the second part and their successors in this trust, shall and may, from out of the funds in their hands, retain a just and reasonable compensation for their services.

And it is further agreed, that the mortgage stamps required by the United States Revenue Laws, instead of being placed on this mortgage, shall be placed on the bonds secured thereby as the same shall be issued.

And the said parties of the second part do hereby severally accept the trusts herein mentioned, and covenant faithfully to administer and execute the same.

In witness whereof, the Southwest Pacific Railroad Company have caused their corporate seal to be hereto affixed, and the same to be signed by John C. Fremont, their President, and William A. Stephens, their Treasurer, for that purpose duly authorized; and the said parties of the second part have hereto set their hands and seals the day and year first above mentioned.

{ Seal S.W.P. R.R. Co. }

Executed and delivered } in presence of

JOHN C. FREMONT, President.
WM. A. STEPHENS, Treasurer.
JOHN P. YELVERTON, Trustee. [seal.]
CHAS. H. WARD, Trustee. [seal.]

[Subsequent to the various acts hereinbefore mentioned, an act of Congress, approved July 27th, 1866, created the Atlantic and Pacific Railroad Company (with a land grant of about 55,000,-000 of acres to aid in the construction of their road to the Pacific Ocean, by the 35th parallel, as an extension of the Southwest Pacific Railroad), into which the Southwest Pacific Railroad has been consolidated and merged, and which organization partakes of all the rights and powers hitherto possessed by the Southwest Pacific Railroad Company.]